The Wiggle & Giggle BUSY BOOK

The Wiggle & Giggle BUSY BOOK

Trish Kuffner

🅼 Meadowbrook Press

Distributed by Simon & Schuster
New York

Library of Congress Cataloging-in-Publication Data

Kuffner, Trish.
The wiggle & giggle busy book : 365 fun, physical activities for toddlers and preschoolers /
by Trish Kuffner.
p. cm.
Includes index.
ISBN 0-88166-483-9 (Meadowbrook) ISBN 0-684-03135-3 (Simon & Schuster)
1. Movement education. 2. Education, Primary—Activity programs. 3. Early childhood
education—Parent participation. I. Title: Wiggle and giggle busy book. II. Title: 365
fun, physical activities for toddlers and preschoolers. III. Title: Three hundred sixty five
fun, physical activities for toddlers and preschoolers. IV. Title.
GV452.K82 2005
372.86'8—dc22
                                   2004021303

Editorial Director: Christine Zuchora-Walske
Editor: Megan McGinnis
Proofreader: Angela Wiechmann
Production Manager: Paul Woods
Graphic Design Manager: Tamara Peterson
Cover Art: Dorothy Stott
Illustrations: Laurel Aiello

Published by Meadowbrook Press, 5451 Smetana Drive, Minnetonka, Minnesota 55343

www.meadowbrookpress.com

BOOK TRADE DISTRIBUTION by Simon and Schuster, a division of Simon and Schuster, Inc.,
1230 Avenue of the Americas, New York, New York 10020

10 09 08 07 06   10 9 8 7 6 5 4 3

Printed in the United States of America

Dedication

For Janine Willemsen, my running partner, kindred spirit, and dearest friend. Although South Africa calls you home, your legacy will be with me at every step I run and finishing line I cross. You are an inspiration to all who know you.

Contents

Introduction

When I began writing *The Wiggle & Giggle Busy Book* a year ago, I thought it would be like the other books in my Busy Book series. I designed those books to help parents and caregivers cope with the demands of toddlers and preschoolers (and their short attention spans); keep kids busy with creative games and activities; and give parents and caregivers simple, straightforward ideas that don't require major organization or cleanup.

While writing this book, however, I discovered some alarming statistics. In North America, the number of overweight and obese children has doubled or even tripled in the last twenty years. And these statistics no longer apply just to North America. Obesity, diabetes, and heart disease, once thought to be diseases of the wealthy, are spreading to developing countries. Poor diet and inactivity are now global problems.

Clearly, this book isn't just for parents who want ideas on how to channel their overactive children's energy. Instead, because I believe that increasing physical activity and fitness levels in early childhood is essential for the health and well-being of the next generation, this book is for parents and caregivers of toddlers and preschoolers of every shape, size, and energy level. Our attitudes toward exercise and fitness take shape early in life, and parents and caregivers of toddlers and preschoolers are in the best position to ensure that children lead healthy, active lifestyles and learn the importance of physical fitness.

In fact, this book may not even make parents' lives simpler, as I hope my previous books have done. For today's busy families, I know that it sometimes seems easier for parents and caregivers to let their young ones watch TV, play computer games, or otherwise keep themselves occupied with sedentary activities, but kids need to move! Kids who are active develop physical skills, which contribute to cognitive, social, and emotional development. Kids who are active perceive themselves to be competent, and kids who feel good about their physical abilities are more likely to participate in activities necessary to improve health and fitness.

Many parents worry that they're not qualified to teach their kids physical skills, that unless children are taught the "right" way to move, they'll be at a disadvantage. Of course that's not true! Certainly teachers and coaches who wish to teach a particular skill must focus on proper technique, but parents and caregivers don't need to be experts in order to instill in their children the importance of physical activity. It's not as important that children know the "right" techniques as it is they enjoy being active. Keep in mind that kids who are active throughout their preschool years—even without formal training in movement skills—will have an advantage over those who've spent a majority of their time doing sedentary activities. I've designed the ideas in *The Wiggle & Giggle Busy Book* with this fact in mind, and I've made it easy for you and your child to have fun and be active together.

While the ideas in this book are great for getting adults to be active with their children, they won't do much to get most adults in shape. If you lead a fairly sedentary life yourself and wonder if you've got what it takes to raise an active child, know that it's never too late to get physically fit. Several years past my fortieth birthday, I discovered the joy of being active. I started out taking long walks and short runs and eventually graduated to five- to ten-mile runs three or four times a week. I recently ran a half marathon, and I hope to have a full marathon under my belt by the time this book is published. I'm not an elite athlete by any stretch of the imagination, just an average middle-age mom who has learned to love the exhilaration of pushing myself beyond what I think I can do. (Starting my day with an hour or two of uninterrupted girl talk with my running partner and closest friend is pretty motivating, too!)

Some ideas in *The Wiggle & Giggle Busy Book* appear in other books I've written, and I've included them to provide the best physical activities and games for young children. I've organized the activities by chapter, but many of them can fit into two or more chapters. For example, many indoor activities make great outdoor activities, and a few seasonal materials turn creative movement activities into indoor holiday games.

The abilities of toddlers and preschoolers vary greatly, so some ideas in this book will be too advanced for a young toddler, while others will be too simple for an older preschooler. Because a child's development often isn't related to his age, I don't suggest ages for most of the activities. Choose activities that best meet your child's capabilities and interests. If a new activity doesn't go over well, don't write it off altogether. Try it again later, or vary the activity to make it more meaningful and interesting for your child.

My hope for *The Wiggle & Giggle Busy Book* is that it'll help children (and the adults who love them) learn to love physical activity and become fit for life. Whether you lead an active lifestyle or are planning to lead one very soon, my wish is that this book will give you the right combination of motivation, information, and ideas to help you raise a child who is healthy, strong, flexible, and on the road to lifelong fitness. If you have any questions or comments about this book, you can e-mail me or write to me in care of Meadowbrook Press. I'd love to hear from you.

Trish

P.S. In recognition of the fact that children do indeed come in both sexes, and in an effort to represent each, the use of masculine and feminine pronouns will alter with each chapter.

Chapter 1

Wiggle, Giggle, and Move!

Mama exhorted her children at every opportunity
to 'jump at de sun.' We might not land on the sun,
but at least we would get off the ground.

—Zora Neale Hurston

Children are born to wiggle and giggle! Watch your toddler
for a moment or two, and her boundless energy will amaze you.
Whether she's eating, playing, singing, bathing, or listening to
a story or song, she'll likely be squirming and fidgeting, making sure she's not missing anything that's happening around
her. While preschoolers usually have slightly longer attention
spans, they also have lots of energy, often making their
parents wish they'd sit still for a while!

But if children are born to move, why are more and more
of them growing up without the proper strength and physical
development to take on new learning challenges? Obesity rates in
young children are about six times higher than they were forty
years ago. Diagnoses of asthma and diabetes in children are
rising, and cardiologists are seeing fatty streaks—a risk factor
for coronary heart disease—in children as young as age two.
(See http://www.kid-fit.com/news.htm for more information.)

To what can we attribute these alarming statistics? As parents,
it's easy to imagine that our kids are active enough because of

our own memories of active childhoods. But our children's daily lives are quite different from what ours were as children. In the article "The Issues: Physically Active for Life," published on the PBS TeacherSource website, Dr. Steve Sanders, Chair of the Department of Health and Physical Education at Tennessee Technological University, believes that the reasons are cultural. He writes, "Over the past forty years, our culture has changed dramatically. Once a physically active nation, our society now actually discourages physical activity. Our communities are centered on the automobile, discouraging walking and bicycling by children. Because of concerns about safety, children spend less time outside playing. New technology (TV, computers, hand-held children's electronic games) conditions young people to be less active."

In addition, many parents and caregivers want to spend their children's toddler and preschool years helping them develop the skills that will better prepare them for academics. Parents and caregivers read books and articles for ideas on teaching their children arts and crafts, cooking, music, reading, and more. Even many preschool programs emphasize traditional academics over physical activity. As a result, young children may spend most of their waking hours engaged in activities that require them to sit still for too long or perform such skills as writing the alphabet with pencils before they have the strength and coordination in their hands and fingers to do so correctly. Parents and caregivers need to proactively provide opportunities that strengthen their children's bodies from the time little ones are very young.

What about kids who are anything but sedentary? Perhaps your child never seems to stop! While she may exhaust you at times, be thankful that she's active and energetic. She may get all the exercise she needs just from playing around the home, but energy levels don't necessarily indicate fitness. As Mary Mayesky writes in *Creative Activities for Young Children*, "Many parents and teachers believe that simply providing children with free play opportunities is all the support children need to grow healthy bodies and develop motor skills. While free play is important, it does not guarantee skill development beyond the minimal performance level." And in his book *Active for Life*, Dr. Steve Sanders writes, "Active play, though important, does not by itself ensure that children acquire key physical skills."

Now, I don't believe that these professionals' warnings mean that you must teach your child the "right" techniques for these physical skills. Rather, I believe they mean that you need to incorporate all kinds of physical activity into your child's daily life. For example, your child may spend most of her day running around the house and yard, but that won't help her learn to kick or throw a ball. All children, even energetic ones, need direction to develop a wide range of specific physical skills.

Whether your child is naturally active or needs encouragement to move her feet, incorporating the activities from *The*

Wiggle & Giggle Busy Book into her daily life will help her develop an active lifestyle and acquire the physical skills she needs for her school years and beyond. Physically active children have a greater chance of being healthy for a lifetime, and that's a goal worth striving for!

Benefits of Physical Activity

Whatever your age, regular exercise improves your quality of life and helps prevent disease. Physical activity also benefits your child in the following ways:

- Regular physical activity improves your child's general health. Daily activity strengthens her heart and respiratory system and helps maintain healthy bones, muscles, and joints. (No matter how much milk your child drinks, the necessary calcium won't get into her bones without regular weight-bearing activities like walking, running, or skipping.)
- Regular physical activity improves your child's appearance. Exercise helps control weight, build lean muscle, reduce fat, promote good posture and balance, and maintain flexibility.
- Physical activity enhances the development of movement skills. Active children develop locomotor skills (running, jumping, skipping, and so on) at younger ages than less active children, a key factor in successful performance of these skills later on.

- Participation in physical activities enhances self-esteem. Playing active games and doing physical activities fosters enjoyment and satisfaction, increases relaxation, and reinforces a good self-image.
- Being active with others encourages a sense of community. Participating in active games and activities with others helps children meet new friends as well as develop and strengthen language, social, and problem-solving skills.
- Regular physical activity helps instill a love of movement and exercise. Children who engage regularly in physical activity and find it fun and enjoyable are well on their way to establishing lifelong fitness.

Physical Activity for Toddlers and Preschoolers

Several years ago, the National Association of Sports & Physical Education (NASPE) released physical activity guidelines for infants and toddlers. The association developed the guidelines not only to combat the rising rates of childhood obesity, but also to address the correct physical and cognitive development of infants, toddlers, and preschoolers. Many professionals believe that the amount of time very young children spend in car seats, strollers, and in other confining apparatuses delays developmental milestones, like rolling over, climbing, and hand-eye coordination. These experts recommend that parents include daily physical activity in their children's lives starting at birth.

The NASPE guidelines for toddlers and preschoolers are as follows:

- Toddlers should do at least thirty minutes of structured physical activity each day; preschoolers, at least sixty minutes.
- Toddlers and preschoolers should do at least sixty minutes each day of unstructured physical activity and shouldn't be sedentary for more than sixty minutes at a time except when sleeping.
- Toddlers should develop movement skills (for example, jumping in place) that are building blocks for more complex movement tasks; preschoolers should master movement skills (for example, galloping rhythmically and steadily) that are building blocks for more complex movement tasks.
- Toddlers and preschoolers should have indoor and outdoor areas that meet or exceed recommended safety standards for performing large muscle activities.
- Those caring for toddlers and preschoolers should be aware of the importance of physical activity and facilitate the children's movement skills.

Does this mean that toddlers and preschoolers should participate in structured, scheduled exercise sessions? In *Kid Fitness*, Dr. Kenneth Cooper writes, "Although I'm a great advocate of kid fitness, I'm also a great *opponent* of rushing very young children into exercises or sports for which they are ill-suited, either physically or emotionally." For infants, he recommends a safe, nurturing, and minimally structured play environment. Parents should encourage older children (up to age seven) to participate in vigorous aerobic activities, like tag, chase, random running, racing, swimming, cycling, and walking. In addition, jumping rope, climbing trees, and playing on playground equipment are great ways to build muscle strength and stamina.

Simply put, toddlers and preschoolers need to do straightforward, age-appropriate activities every day to help them learn to walk, run, and eventually do all the other movements adults often take for granted. The goal is to make physical activity a part of your child's daily life—a goal that the commonsense, fun activities in *The Wiggle & Giggle Busy Book* will help you reach.

A Parent's or Caregiver's Role

You may think that children just naturally learn to move, but this isn't always the case. For example, a baby who spends most of her time in a car seat may not learn to crawl. A toddler who lives in an apartment may not learn to climb stairs. Or a preschooler who spends too much time doing sedentary activities may not develop the stamina needed for more active play. The development of these children probably isn't delayed for any physical reason; rather, the children's environment is usually the cause for the delay, which means parents and caregivers play a very important role in helping children learn to move. Jane Clark, a movement specialist at the University of Maryland, says that parents "have to provide that environment that hooks the brain up to the muscles." Just as we teach children basic health and safety habits, we must also teach them how to develop active, healthy ways to use their bodies.

Here are some simple ways to teach your child that physical activity is important...and fun!

- Be fit and healthy yourself. As the saying goes, attitudes and beliefs are caught more than taught. If your child sees you regularly exercising, running, dancing, and so on, she'll realize that fitness is an important and enjoyable part of life.
- Be active with your child. Take an interest in her fitness and help her foster an appreciation for an active, healthy lifestyle. Plan activities together. Go for walks; go to the park to swing, climb, and slide; go for bike rides; go swimming; play catch; play tag or race. Have your child help you garden or do yard work.
- Make physical activity a part of daily life. Emphasize the fun and enjoyment of exercise, but never force your child to do a physical activity or use it as punishment.
- Develop a "long cut" mentality rather than a "shortcut" mentality. Park farther away, take the stairs instead of the elevator, and walk to do your errands or go to a friend's house. These are just a few easy ways you can incorporate physical activity into your day.

- Help your child develop a positive attitude about exercise. Watch out for negative messages about fitness. Send only positive verbal and nonverbal messages about fitness to your child.
- Limit the amount of time your child watches TV or plays computer or video games. Sedentary activities like these should be the exception, not the rule. Go on short hikes, take bike rides, or do other family activities that will draw your child away from the TV and computer.
- Encourage healthy eating habits. Physical activity requires proper nutrition. Carrot sticks, apples, crackers, and pretzels are much better snacks than cookies, soda, and chips. You'll definitely need to model good eating habits, because we know that the behaviors children see most often at home are the ones they'll likely adopt for life.
- Choose activities that encourage cooperation and personal challenge instead of competition. Children who are at a disadvantage may become frustrated and give up physical activity altogether if they're directly competing with more capable children.
- Help your child feel good about her abilities. Be positive and enthusiastic about the tasks she can accomplish. Encourage improvement gently. Remind her that, above all, physical activity should be fun.
- Ensure your child has a safe environment in which to play.

- Dress her for active play and let her know it's okay to get dirty. Always check that your child's shoes and clothing won't stop her from being active.

Parents' influence doesn't diminish as children grow up; on the contrary, parents continue to play a big role in shaping their children's attitudes toward fitness. In *Your Child's Fitness*, Susan Kalish writes that kids dislike fitness and sports when they feel that winning is most important, when they feel that their performances never improve, or when they feel that they don't have a say in the sports they play. Other reasons that kids dislike fitness include getting injured too often, feeling forced to play through pain, doing the same thing over and over, and being ridiculed by friends, family, or a coach. Kids enjoy fitness when they have fun, feel successful, play with peers, experience a variety of activities, share these activities with family members, have an enthusiastic coach or teacher (or parent), and feel that having an active lifestyle is their decision, not their parents'.

Getting Started

Getting fit with your child isn't difficult if you think of physical activity as play—and play is fun! Play helps build all the skills children need for the future: playing house helps build imaginative and social skills; playing card games helps build cognitive skills; playing with play dough helps build small motor skills; and playing active games helps build movement skills. If you feel daily physical activity is important for you and your family, and if you can make exercise a part of your daily routine, you're well on your way to giving your child the means for lifelong health. Here are ways to get started:

- Gather some basic equipment. You don't need many supplies for most of the activities in this book. You can use balls, Hula-Hoops, beanbags, rope, buckets, and racquets in many ways and in many different activities. You can use Hula-Hoops as targets, bases, safe zones, or as something to throw, catch, or move through. You can throw, roll, kick, bounce, or dribble balls. You can use racquets to propel or deflect objects. You can even use everyday objects like milk cartons, bleach bottles, or ice-cream buckets to throw or catch objects.

- Make a Crazy Activity Can. Make a list of physical activities that require no special equipment, no preparation, and little adult participation or supervision. For example, set a timer for one minute and have your preschooler climb the stairs, throw beanbags or individually wrapped toilet paper rolls into a laundry basket, or jump off a step stool. Write these ideas on separate index cards or slips of paper and put them in an empty coffee can. If you like, cover the can with cheerful contact paper, or cover it with plain paper and have your child decorate it with paints, markers, or crayons. When your child has energy to burn, or when she's sat still just a little too long, choose a card from the can for some instant activity.

- Make a weekly activity plan. Many parents find it helpful to plan their activities a week in advance. Read through this book and make a list of activities you'd like to try with your child. Use a calendar or planner to create a weekly activity plan, making sure to include a variety of indoor and outdoor activities. Gather all your equipment and supplies ahead of time so you're ready to go when your child is.
- Start a family exercise program, such as walking or cycling three or more times a week. In *Kid Fitness*, Dr. Kenneth Cooper advises parents to schedule regular aerobic activity sessions five to seven days a week. For children up to age seven, Dr. Cooper suggests a program that involves increasing the time spent each day in aerobic exercise from five minutes to thirty minutes over a ten-week period.
- Measure your family's fitness levels. If you like, measure these levels every month or two. Give each family member a chart on which to record measurements and note improvements. For young children, measure the distance they can run in one or two minutes, the number of times they can bounce a ball, the number of jumps they can do in one minute, and so on. For older children and adults, measure the distance they can run in ten minutes, the number of pushups they can do in two minutes, the numbers of laps they can swim, and so on. Emphasize individual improvement; don't make achievements a competition among family members. Everyone should have fun and no one should push themselves beyond his or her body's limitations.

No matter how you choose to include physical activity in your child's life, remember that the activities you choose should burn energy, let your child develop movement skills, and most of all, be fun for both you and your child. The activities in this book are a great place to start.

About This Book

The 365 ideas in *The Wiggle & Giggle Busy Book* will help your child be active, have fun, and learn to move in a variety of ways. I've organized the book so you can easily find ideas for active play outdoors or indoors. I've also included ideas for creative movement, for water play, and for holidays like Valentine's Day, Easter, Hanukkah, and more. The wide range of ideas will help your child develop the important skills listed on the next page:

- Locomotor skills: These skills let your child move from place to place. Some examples include walking, running, hopping, skipping, galloping, sliding, leaping, climbing, and crawling.
- Stability skills: Your child will benefit from turning, twisting, bending, stopping, rolling, and jumping because these skills help her develop good balance and stability and help her better perform and enjoy other motor skills.
- Manipulative skills: These skills will help your child learn to throw, catch, kick, punt, dribble, volley, and strike.

Each chapter includes activities that are appropriate for groups of young children. These group activities will help kids develop a variety of locomotor, stability, and manipulative skills.

What about Small Motor Skills?

Teachers who work with young children are finding that more and more kids are beginning school without the proper strength and physical development to take on new learning challenges. While the development of large motor skills is very important, children also need to develop their small motor skills to successfully learn to write, cut, pick up small objects, button and zipper clothing, and so on. Make sure your child spends some time each day doing activities that help develop her hand and finger strength, hand-eye coordination, and perceptual skills. Here are some ideas:

- Kneading bread dough or pizza dough
- Squeezing water-filled sponges
- Playing with play dough or modeling clay
- Squirting a spray bottle filled with water
- Playing with nesting blocks
- Playing with building blocks
- Stringing O-shaped cereal on thread or string or making collages out of edible objects
- Stringing beads on thread or string
- Doing finger plays
- Drawing designs on plates covered with whipped cream, pudding, or other edible material
- Finger-painting
- Putting together simple jigsaw puzzles

For additional ideas on small motor activities for toddlers and preschoolers, look for the other books I've written for this age group: *The Toddler's Busy Book*, *The Preschooler's Busy Book*, *The Arts and Crafts Busy Book*, and *Picture Book Activities*.

Let's Get Moving!

Daily physical activity plays an incredibly important role in your child's development and helps prepare her for the challenges her school years will bring. To be sure your child gets off to the best physical start, model a fit and healthy lifestyle yourself and give your child lots of opportunities to move and play. Don't force your child beyond her ability, and remember to provide lots of encouragement. Above all, keep it fun!

Raising healthy, happy, productive children requires physical activity, so whenever you can, wiggle, giggle, run, jump, climb, skip, and move with your child. She's worth it!

Chapter 2
Outdoor Activities

*A man too busy to take care of his health
is like a mechanic too busy to take care of his tools.*

—Spanish proverb

What better place for a young child to move his body than
the outdoors! Most toddlers and preschoolers never tire of
running, jumping, skipping, and climbing in the fresh air.
They love discovering all the ways they can use their developing motor skills. In addition to the mental and physical health
benefits everyone gets from spending time outdoors, most
parents will agree that playing outside with your kids just
feels great!

Whether it's warm or cold, wet or dry, windy or calm, try to
play outdoors with your child every day. Take him to the playground, walk in the rain, play games in the backyard, pick
wildflowers, fly a kite, throw snowballs, watch him ride his
tricycle—the possibilities are endless.

The following games and activities will give your child
opportunities to develop his basic movement skills. Introduce
games and activities one at a time so he doesn't become over-
whelmed. Most of them will be fun and entertaining for him,
but some may be challenging. If your child finds a game or
activity too difficult, try it again when he's more capable.

Remember that while practicing skills is important, having fun and being active together are the most important reasons to do any game or activity with your child.

Locomotor Activities

Most kids won't need much encouragement to move when they're outdoors, especially when playing in a park or playground. Some children, however, may prefer more sedentary activities, like playing in a sandbox, to more active ones, like walking, running, climbing, or crawling. Though your child doesn't need to be active all the time while outdoors, even a simple walk will help develop his locomotor skills. If your child is reluctant to walk, motivate him to do so: count red cars as you walk; collect fallen leaves, rocks, or shells; or have races along the way. Use the following activities to help encourage your child to develop his locomotor skills.

Basic Hopscotch

Chalk

OUT
10
9
8
7
6
5
4
3
2
1

Use chalk to draw a basic hopscotch court (like the one illustrated) on pavement. Have your child hop up the court and back again, hopping in each space both up and back. On the first trip, he hops on his right foot. On the second trip, he hops on his left foot. On his third trip, he hops on alternating feet. On the fourth trip, he hops with his feet together. Your child hops in this sequence until he makes a mistake like hopping on a line, putting both feet down when he's supposed to be hopping on one foot, or hopping on the wrong foot, at which point he fouls out. Then you take a turn hopping in the same way.

When it's your child's turn again, he starts hopping from where he fouled out on his last turn. The winner is the first player to finish the entire sequence of hops.

Riding Toys

Chalk
Riding toy or wagon

Use chalk to draw a path or roadway on pavement. If you like, draw stop signs, crossroads, and other roadway details. Have your child ride his toy or push or pull his wagon along the path or road.

Toddler Triathlon

Set up a triathlon course to challenge your toddler.

Rope
Tricycle
Wading pool

Make a start line with the rope. Place the wading pool at the beginning of the course, and park a tricycle several feet from the pool. Have your toddler run from the start line to the tricycle. Have him hop on the tricycle and ride back to the pool. Have him "swim" (crawl) through the water from one side of the pool to the other to finish the race.

Variation: Divide a group of children equally into two or more teams and have a relay race, using one tricycle and pool for each team.

Wings

Several 2-foot strips of crepe paper
Tape

Have your child wear a long-sleeved shirt or jacket. Along the backs of the sleeves, tape the crepe paper strips so they hang down. If you like, do the same to your sleeves. Then run around outside and flap your wings. Be sure to make birdcalls as you "fly" together!

Circle Walk

You don't have to go far when you go for a walk with your child—just walk in a circle in your backyard or at the park. To prevent dizziness, reverse the direction you're walking every now and then. Try the following actions as you walk together:
• Swing your arms forward and back.
• Stretch your arms overhead and walk on tiptoe.
• Squat and walk like a duck.
• Roll your head from shoulder to shoulder.
• Shrug your shoulders.
• Rotate your arms like a windmill.
• Walk fast then slow down; speed up and slow down.

I Spy

Play this game with your preschooler in your yard, at the park, or as you take a walk together.

Tell your child, "I spy, with my little eye, something that is green (or round, skinny, tall, or whatever)." Give him a few moments to look around, then count from ten to zero while he runs to touch something with that feature before you reach zero. Take turns spying and running.

Variation: Have your child hop, skip, or gallop instead of run.

Snake in the Grass

4 rubber snakes (or beanbags or small plastic toys)

Have your child stand on the far side of the yard and close his eyes. Hide the snakes in the grass in different places around the yard. When you yell, "Snake in the grass!" your child must run and find the snakes. Have him bring them to you before they slither away!

Grid Challenge

Washable paint, chalk, or masking tape

Mark a two-by-five-foot rectangle on pavement. Divide the rectangle into ten one-foot squares and number each square from zero to nine. You can write the numbers in order or randomly, but make sure two sequential numbers are never more than one square apart.

Challenge your child to do the following actions:

- Step on each number in order from zero to nine.
- Hop on each number in order from nine to zero.
- Jump with two feet on each number in order from zero to nine.
- Hop backward on each number in order from nine to zero.
- Jump on only even numbers.
- Hop on only odd numbers.

0	1	4	7	9
2	3	6	5	8

Variation: Older children may enjoy hopping out dates, telephone numbers, or solutions to simple addition and subtraction problems. For very young children, use shapes or colors instead of numbers.

Outdoor Obstacle Course

Various outdoor objects
Stopwatch (optional)

Use the outdoor objects to create an obstacle course for your child to run through. For example, plan the course around a tree stump he can jump over. Have him crawl under a patio table, hop down a hopscotch court, jump up and down in a sandbox, swing on a swing, climb up the ladder to a slide then slide down, and so on. Have him run through the course in one direction, then have him run through it again in the opposite direction. You can time him, or he can race against siblings or friends.

Caution: Do not use objects that have sharp corners or that can tip over easily. If necessary, cushion objects with pillows and blankets.

Roller Coaster Walk

Have fun with your child imitating a roller coaster as you walk together. Walk low to the ground, then high, then low again. Walk slowly, then speed up to a run. Continue varying your position and speed until your child tires of this activity. For fun, raise and lower your voices as you go up and down the roller coaster.

Disappearing Playground

Paintbrush
Bucket of water
Trike, bike, or scooter (optional)
Sidewalk chalk or biodegradable tempera paint
Garden hose (optional)

- Have your child dip the paintbrush in water and use it to draw large shapes or pictures on the driveway or sidewalk. Give him directions such as, "Walk to the square," "Hop to the circle," or "Run to the flower." Play until the images disappear.
- Dip the paintbrush in water and draw a hopscotch court on the driveway or sidewalk. Play hopscotch with your child, or just have fun jumping from square to square.
- Dip the paintbrush in water and draw a curvy trail for your child to follow. Have him walk, run, hop, or ride his trike, bike, or scooter along the trail.
- Have your child use sidewalk chalk or biodegradable tempera paint to draw or write in one of the above ways. When you're done, use a bucket of water or a garden hose to wash the chalk or paint away.

Blowing Bubbles

Bubble solution
Bubble wand

On a nice day, go outside with your child and blow some bubbles. Have your child chase, catch, stomp, clap, and poke them. Take turns blowing and chasing the bubbles.

Tag

Tag is a great game to play with your child outdoors. It doesn't require any equipment, can be played with any number of players, and is enjoyed by children of all ages. Here are a few variations to try:

- Shadow Tag: On a bright sunny day, have your child try tagging players' shadows.
- Water Tag: Have your child tag players by tossing water balloons at them or hitting them with a stream from a water gun.
- Turtle Tag: Players are safe from being tagged when they roll on their backs and wave their arms and legs in the air like overturned turtles.
- Toilet Tag: Players are safe from being tagged when they squat as though on a toilet. (Preschool boys especially seem to appreciate this hilarious variation.)

Fly a Kite

Your preschooler will have so much fun flying a kite, he won't focus on how much he's running to keep it aloft.

Kite (store-bought or homemade)
Balloon on a string (optional)

- On a warm, slightly windy day, have your child fly a kite in a park.
- A toddler will enjoy "flying" a balloon on a string. Encourage your toddler to pretend it's a windy day, and have him chase the balloon as it "blows" this way and that.

Caution: Balloon pieces can pose an extreme choking hazard for very young children, so any balloon play must be carefully supervised.

Walk in the Dark

Flashlight (optional)

On a mild, clear evening, bundle yourself and your child in reflective or light-colored clothing and take a walk in the dark. If possible, carry a flashlight and use it in the following activities.

- Shine the flashlight beam on a spot several feet in front of your child and have him jump with feet together toward the spot.
- Shine the flashlight beam in a random path on the ground and have your child run after the beam.
- Make circles on the ground with the flashlight beam and have your child skip around the circle.

Bring a stroller or wagon to carry a tired toddler, stop for a snack if you like, then amble home to a bedtime story.

Backing Up

Challenge your child to see how many ways he can move backward. (This challenge may be difficult for young toddlers, but older preschoolers will enjoy it.) Try one or more of the following movements:

- walking
- running
- hopping
- crawling
- skipping
- scooting along on his bottom
- crab-walking

Running Challenge

Stopwatch (optional)

Have fun with your child by running in one or more of the
following ways:
- Mark a start line and a finish line. Run the distance as
  quickly as possible. If you like, time your child and
  challenge him to run faster.
- Run the same distance as slowly as possible. How slowly
  can he run before he's walking?
- Begin running very slowly then gradually run faster.
- Begin running quickly then gradually slow down to a stop.

Rope Spiral

Rope, several feet long

Make a pathway by laying the rope in a spiral with coils that
are about eighteen inches apart. How many ways can your
child move along the path between the coils? Try walking,
running, hopping, skipping, crawling, and so on.

Variation: Lay two ropes on the ground so they're parallel to
each other and make a zigzag or curved pathway. Your child
must move along the path in various ways.

Puddle Fun

Your child will enjoy some puddle fun after a rainstorm or, better yet, while it's still raining! Put on your boots and raincoats and carry umbrellas, if you like. Chant "Rain, Rain Go Away" or sing rain songs as you run, hop, skip, and stomp through the puddles.

Caution: If it's still raining, make certain there are no signs of lightning before you head outdoors.

Leader Tag

Before you begin the game, determine a safe zone in your yard. Then have your child hop, skip, crawl, or move any way he likes around the play area as you follow him and copy his movements. Whenever he likes, he can call out "Tag!" and try to tag you before you reach the safe zone. If he tags you, he copies your movements during the next round of play. If not, you follow his movements for another round.

Limbo

Rope

Recruit another person to hold one end of a rope while you hold the other. Hold the rope at a height so your child can walk under it without touching it. Lower the rope an inch or two, and have your child crouch slightly and pass under it without touching it. Continue lowering the rope each time he attempts to pass under it. Eventually he'll have to inch under it on his back or tummy.

Variation: Start with the rope on the ground, then raise it slightly each time your child jumps over it.

Hop, Skip, Jump

Penny or other coin

While on a walk with your child in your neighborhood, flip a penny to determine what action he'll do. For example, if "heads" comes up, your child will run; if "tails," he'll hop or skip. Change the action often to include movement skills like walking backward or on tiptoe, walking heel-to-toe, jumping and landing on both feet, hopping on one foot, and so on.

Sled Pull

Sleds aren't just for the snow.
Bring out your sleds for some
outdoor fun with your
child in any season!

Sleds
Dolls or plush animals

- Load up your sleds with dolls or plush animals. Pretend to be horses pulling carriages or sleds behind you.
- For two or more children, have a race to see who can be the first to load up a sled and pull it to a finish line.
- For a group of children, form two or more teams and have a relay race with sleds.

Stability Activities

The following activities are fun to do with your child and will help develop his stability skills. Start with simple balance activities, like standing on one leg and balancing on a wide, stable base. Then try more challenging ones, like balancing on a narrow, unstable base. Have your child balance on objects at low heights before having him try to balance on objects at higher heights. Follow your child closely so you're ready to steady him if he wavers. Once your child masters these stability activities, challenge him to try them while balancing an object (like a beanbag) on his head or outstretched hand.

For more stability activities, see pages 115–138. Many of these activities for indoor play are also suitable for outdoor play.

Rope Games

Rope

- Lay a long rope in a pattern on your deck or the grass. Try a zigzag pattern, circle, square, or other shape. Have your child walk along the rope.
- Lay the rope in a closed shape like a circle or square. Have your child think of how many ways he can move in and out of the shape. Try stepping in and out, jumping, somersaulting, and so on.
- Lay the rope in a straight line and ask your child to think of how many ways he can go over it: walk across it, hop over it (on one or two feet), jump across it, crawl across it, and so on.

Frog Jump

Chalk or several Hula-Hoops or ropes

Draw circles on the pavement with chalk. Or on the ground, lay Hula-Hoops or make circles with ropes. Space the circles so your child can jump easily from one to the next. Have your child stand inside one of the circles and prepare to jump to another "pond." Encourage him to bend his knees, swing his arms, and jump, landing on both feet at the same time.

Steady Now

This activity is great for older preschoolers.

Short step stool, sturdy plastic crate, or piece
  of wood several inches thick and wide
Soft ball

Have your child stand on a short step stool. How many movements can he make without falling off? Have him try standing on one foot, turning around, bending to pick up an object on the stool, jumping up and down, crouching into a ball, swaying, and so on. Throw a soft ball to him and see if he can catch it without falling off.

Zigzag Walks

Chalk
Beanbag

On the pavement, draw a long line that has straight and zigzag sections. If you like, add curved or wavy sections. Have your child walk along the line. When he reaches the end, have him stop then walk backward, trying to stay on the line. How fast can he walk without walking off the line? Have him hop on one or two feet along the line. Can he walk quickly while balancing a beanbag on his head?

Rope Turn

8-foot rope
Rubber ball and sock (optional)

Stand about five or six feet away from your child. Hold one end of the rope in your hand near the ground. Turn around and around like the second hand of a clock. Have your child jump over the rope as it reaches him.

Variation: To weight the rope, place a rubber ball into a sock, then tie one end of the rope around the sock above the ball.

Skipping Rope

Rope

Tie one end of a rope to a tree or other stable object. Hold the other end and slowly swing it back and forth.

- Have your child practice jumping over the rope as it swings toward him.
- When your child is comfortable jumping over the rope, have him try jumping several times in a row as you swing the rope back and forth. How many jumps can he make?
- When your child can jump over the rope easily, see if he can jump over it when you fully turn it (rotate it overhead and underfoot with each turn) instead of swinging it back and forth.

Ladder Walk

Wooden or metal ladder
Beanbag or other small lightweight object (optional)
Short step stool (optional)

Lay the ladder on the grass. Have your child try the following activities:

- Starting at one end of the ladder, walk between each rung, turn around at the end, and return to the starting point.
- Starting at one end of the ladder, walk on the rungs, turn at the end, and return to the starting point. Have your child stretch out his arms to the side and balance as he walks.
- Place a beanbag at one end of the ladder. Have your child start from the other end and walk on the rungs to the beanbag, pick it up and place it on his head, turn around, and walk back to the starting point.
- Place one end of the ladder on a short step stool. Have your child start from the end on the ground, walk on the rungs to the end, then turn around and come back to the starting point. Follow your child closely so you're ready to steady him if he wavers.

Long Jump

Rope or string
Penny or marker (milk jug lid or bingo chip)
Tape measure (optional)

Mark a start line with rope or string. Have your child stand at the line and jump forward as far as he can. Place a penny to mark where he landed, then have him jump again. If his second jump is farther than his first, move the penny to the new spot; otherwise, leave the penny where it is. Have your child jump five times, leaving his marker at the farthest jump. If you like, use a tape measure to measure his farthest jump.

Log Roll

Find a grassy gentle slope that's free of rocks and other objects. Have your child lie on the grass at the top of the slope, his arms crossed over his chest, and roll down like a log.

Shadows

On a sunny day, find an area outside where your child can see his shadow.

- Have him move various body parts to see the shadow shapes he casts.
- Have him try making shadows of various sizes: big, small, wide, and narrow.
- Join hands with your child or have two or more children join hands to cast shadow monsters with your bodies.
- Have him think of an animal and try to make its shape from the shadow his body casts.

Jumping Practice

Sturdy plastic crate or short step stool (optional)

Have your child practice jumping down. Encourage him to jump from a curb or the edge of a sandbox. Practice jumping down from a bottom step or a sturdy plastic crate. Encourage him to land balanced with his feet together.

Dodge the Ball

Large, soft ball

Throw the ball at your child. He must stand in place until you release the ball, then dodge out of the way to avoid being hit. If you like, give a verbal signal as you release the ball, or just have him watch the ball for his cue to move. Change places and let your child try to hit you with the ball.

Jump the River

Chalk
Ropes (optional)

Use chalk to draw two long parallel lines two feet apart on the pavement to make a "river." Draw a few rivers several feet apart from one another. (If you like, use ropes to make the rivers on a grassy area.) Have your child stand on one side of the first river. Show him how to jump across the river, swinging his arms forward as he jumps and landing on both feet on the other side. Have him jump across all the rivers.

Manipulative Activities

Manipulative activities are great to do in your backyard, park, or other outdoor open space. A few balls, beanbags, and a plastic bat or golf club are often all the equipment needed. Toddlers will throw a ball, run after it, pick it up, and throw it again, over and over and over. Preschoolers can practice manipulative skills by throwing balls into a basket or other container, hitting objects with a toy bat or club, and kicking balls toward a target.

Ball Play

Plastic ball
Plastic bat and tee (optional)

- Show your child how to throw a ball overhand. Have him rotate his arm up and back at the shoulder, then quickly bring his arm forward and release the ball, making sure he follows through with the motion.
- Practice catching. Have your child keep his eye on the ball and grab it when it's within reach.
- Practice kicking. Have your child keep his eye on the ball and kick it with the instep of his foot rather than his toe.
- If you like, place a ball on a plastic tee and have your child try to hit the ball with a plastic bat. Pick up the ball and chase your child to a "base"(a tree or other designated point) and then back to "home." You may want to tag your child occasionally, but let him be "safe" sometimes, too.

Ball Dribble

This activity is wonderful for older preschoolers.

Large rubber ball, 1 for each person

On the pavement, have your child stand with one leg slightly forward and one leg behind, as if he's stopped in midstride. Have him bend his knees slightly and hold the ball with one hand on top of it and one hand underneath. Have him release the bottom hand, let the ball bounce, then catch it. Have him continue bouncing the ball in this way until he can do it easily. Have him try to walk, then run, as he does this two-handed bounce. Once he masters this technique, have him try to dribble the ball with only one hand.

Toddler Hockey

Chalk or tape
Toy broom or hockey stick
Plastic hockey puck or jar lid

Use chalk or tape to make circles on pavement. Give your toddler a toy broom or hockey stick and have him use it to push or hit a plastic hockey puck or jar lid into the circles.

Hitting Practice

Yarn or string
Foam ball (for example, a Nerf ball), rolled-up sock,
  or paper bag stuffed with newspaper
Plastic bat
Lightweight paddle or racquet (optional)

Tie one end of the yarn or string around the ball. Tie the other end to a tree branch so the ball hangs at your child's eye level. Have your child use a plastic bat to gently hit the ball. Encourage him to keep his eye on the ball and tap it gently when it returns after each hit.

Variation: Use a lightweight paddle or racquet instead of a bat.

Beanbag Throw

Beanbag
Basket or other container

- Have your child throw a beanbag as high as he can.
  How high can he throw it?
- Have your child toss a beanbag in the air and catch it.
- Throw a beanbag in the air and have your child try to catch it.
- Throw a beanbag in the air and have your child try to catch
  it in a basket.

Sand Play

Sand
Buckets
Wagon
Scoops, muffin pans, funnels, empty plastic soda bottles,
saltshakers, rolling pins, and other items

- Let your child fill up buckets with sand and dump them out again.
- Have him fill up buckets with sand, carry them to a wagon, and dump them into the wagon. Let him pull the wagon around the yard. Then let him fill the buckets with sand from the wagon and return it to the sandbox, or simply dump the wagon's load directly into the sandbox.
- Give your child a variety of items to play with in the sandbox. For example, have him scoop sand into empty plastic soda bottles or into saltshakers, then have him pour or sprinkle the sand into the sections of a muffin pan.

Bouncing

Bouncing a ball may seem like a simple activity, but many young children need practice to master it.

Large rubber ball, one for each person
Recording of music with a strong beat (optional)

On the pavement, show your child how to bounce a ball. Have him hold the ball with both hands at waist level, then have him release the ball, let it bounce, and catch it. Remind him to keep his eye on the ball as it bounces.

Variation: Play some music with a strong beat and practice bouncing the ball in time to the music; for example, call out, "Bounce, two, three, four." Calling out the beat may help your child keep time.

Target Practice

Empty plastic soda bottles
Beanbags

Set up the soda bottles on the grass or on a fence or picnic table. Have your child throw beanbags and try to knock over the bottles. Have him throw overhand, underhand, and sidearm. Let him try throwing with more force, then with less force.

Kickball

All the balls you can find
Hula-Hoop or rope (optional)

Gather all the balls you can find: tennis balls, soccer balls, basketballs, beach balls, and so on. If you like, include small balls like golf balls and Ping-Pong balls, too. Try the following activities with your child:

- Line up the balls one foot apart and have your child kick each one. See which one is the easiest to kick, which one travels the farthest, which one goes the highest, and so on.
- On the ground, lay a Hula-Hoop or form a circle with rope a short distance away from your child. Have him try kicking each ball into the circle. If you like, award points for each success.
- Kick each ball against a wall or other solid surface. Can your child kick the balls back to the wall on the rebound?

Crab Kick

Soccer ball

Have your child lean back and ease his hands to the ground so they're in line with his shoulders. Have him raise his bottom off the ground. Place the ball near your child's feet. Have him move his hands and feet to walk like a crab as he kicks the ball to a chosen point.

Variation: A small group of children may enjoy doing this activity while racing against one another. A larger group can form teams and relay race or play a game of crab soccer.

Bull's-Eye!

Chalk or tape
Ball
Balloon or large soft ball (optional)
Plastic bat (optional)

Use chalk or tape to make a target on a fence or outdoor wall. Have your child throw a ball and try to hit the target. Have him try throwing overhand, underhand, and sidearm.

Variation: Have your child try hitting a balloon or large soft ball with a plastic bat toward the target.

Caution: Balloon pieces can pose an extreme choking hazard for very young children, so any balloon play must be carefully supervised.

Beanbag Hike

Hula-Hoop, string, paint, or chalk
Beanbags
Pencil and paper, or pennies or other markers (optional)

Place a Hula-Hoop on the ground, or use string, paint, or chalk to mark a circle. Have your child stand several feet from the circle and face away from it. Tell him to bend at the waist and throw a beanbag between his legs and into the circle. If you like, award points for each throw; for example, award three points for each beanbag that lands completely inside the circle, two points for each that lands mostly in the circle, and one point for each that lands slightly in the circle. Or have your child toss the beanbags continuously, marking each toss with a penny. When he tires of this activity, look at the pennies to see how accurate his tosses were.

Balloon Tennis

Paddles or racquets (homemade or store-bought),
  1 for each person
Balloon or lightweight ball, 1 for each person

Use paddles or racquets to bat a balloon or lightweight ball
back and forth with your child. How many times can you pass
the ball before it lands on the ground? Count out loud each
time you and your child bat the balloon.

Variation: Give a balloon or ball to each player. Who can bat a
balloon or ball in the air the longest?

Caution: Balloon pieces
can pose an extreme
choking hazard for
very young children,
so any balloon play
must be carefully
supervised.

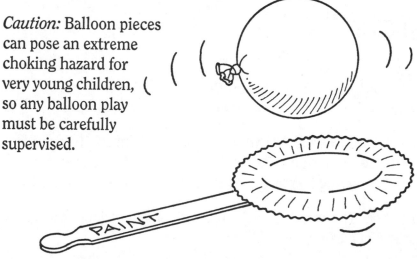

Hit the Moon

Yarn ball or other soft ball
Large rubber ball

Give your child a yarn ball. Throw a large rubber ball (the moon) high into the air. Have your child throw his ball at the moon and try to hit it before it touches the ground.

Variation: For a group activity, have two children throw the rubber ball back and forth while the other children try to hit the moon with their balls.

How Far?

Ball
Small object or string (optional)
Frisbee, lid of an ice-cream pail, or beanbag (optional)

How far can your child throw a ball? Have him try throwing it overhand, underhand, and sidearm. If you like, use a small object or string to mark where the ball lands each time.

Variation: Throw a Frisbee, lid of an ice-cream pail, or beanbag instead of a ball.

Hopscotch Toss

Colored chalk
Beanbag

Use colored chalk to draw shapes in each section
of a hopscotch court; for example, a red heart, a
yellow diamond, a blue circle, and so on. (If you
like, simply draw colored shapes on pavement
rather than on a hopscotch court.) Give your
child a beanbag and have him stand several feet
away from the court. Ask him to hit a specific
shape with each throw; for example, "Please toss
the beanbag onto the blue circle." If you like, instead of shapes
draw pictures or write letters, numbers, or words.

Hit the Ball

Ping-Pong ball
Plastic soda bottle (optional)
Chair or table (optional)
Beanbags or sponges
Kitchen timer

Place a Ping-Pong ball on a fence post, deck railing, or on the mouth of a soda bottle that's placed on a chair or table (fill the bottle with a little water to stabilize it). Have your child stand several feet away from the Ping-Pong ball and try the following activities:

- Throw a beanbag or sponge at the Ping-Pong ball. How many tries does it take before he hits the ball?
- Use a kitchen timer to see if he can hit the ball within a given time period.
- Have him turn around and try to hit the ball by throwing the beanbag or sponge over his shoulder.
- Soak the sponges in water first and have him try to hit the ball with them.
- For a group activity, children can take turns throwing beanbags or sponges to see who can hit the ball first.

Soccer Skills

Soccer balls or rubber balls
Large box (optional)
Foam ball or beach ball (optional)

- Use a soccer ball or rubber ball to practice soccer skills, like kicking, running, trapping, and passing, with your child.
- Turn a large box onto its side and use it as a soccer net. Practice kicking the ball into it.
- If your child is willing to try this move, toss a foam ball or beach ball to him and have him practice hitting it with his head.

Hammer Fun

Toy hammer
Colored golf tees

Let your child use a toy hammer to pound golf tees into your yard. Encourage your child to create a pattern or form a shape like a circle or square with the tees.

Horseshoes

Shovel
Large tin can (empty and clean)
Small beanbags
Pennies or pencil and paper (optional)

Dig a hole in the ground and bury the can so the top of it is flush with the ground. Have your child stand several feet away from the can and hand him a beanbag. Have him throw it and try to get it inside the can. Retrieve the beanbag or hand him another and let him try again. If you like, award pennies or points for each beanbag that lands inside the can.

Wall Ball

Tennis ball

Have your child stand several feet away from a wall. Show him how to throw the ball against the wall, let it bounce once, then catch it. If you like, play with your child. Throw the ball and let him catch it after one bounce, then have him throw the ball and you catch it after one bounce.

Rock Walk

This is a great activity for very young toddlers.

Bucket
Rocks
Hula-Hoop (optional)
Wagon (optional)

Go on a walk with your child. Bring along a bucket and have him collect interesting-looking rocks as you walk. At home, empty the bucket and place it at your child's feet. Hand your child a rock and have him try to drop it into the bucket from the level of his chest. If you like, partly fill the bucket with water first.

Variations:
- Place the bucket several feet away and have your child gently toss the rocks into it.
- Place a Hula-Hoop on the floor and have your child try to toss the rocks into it.
- Have your child place the rocks in a wagon and pull it around the yard.

Golf

Shovel
Large tin can (empty and clean)
Several golf balls
Putter (or toy golf club, narrow length of smooth wood,
*   or heavy cardboard rolled and taped into a "club")*
Pennies or paper and pencil (optional)

Dig a small hole in the ground and bury the tin can so the top of it is flush with the ground. Mark a spot several feet away from the can. This will be the point from which your little golfer will putt.

Give your child the golf balls and a putter. Have him try to putt each ball into the tin can. If you like, award a penny or points for each ball that he putts into the can.

Alligator

Chalk
Beanbag

Draw a large rectangle on the pavement. In the center of the rectangle, draw an alligator. Make the drawing as detailed or as simple as you like. Around the alligator, draw a number of squares; for a toddler, start with four squares, then add more as your child's ability increases. Number each square, or draw a number of objects to represent the numeral, or color each square a different color.

Have your child stand outside the rectangle and toss a beanbag into the squares in numerical order or by specified color. His beanbag can't land on the alligator. If it lands on the alligator, your child must start again from the first square.

Sand Ball

This game is great fun at the beach!

Moist sand
Bucket (optional)

Show your child how to gather the sand in his hands and press it together to form a ball. Place a bucket or draw a circle or other target in the sand. Have your child stand several feet away from the target and throw the sand ball. If you like, award points for each sand ball that hits the target. See how many points he can earn.

Clean Sweep

Toy rake
Broom (optional)

Give your child a toy rake and have him rake leaves, straw, sand, rocks, and other natural debris. If you like, give him a broom and have him sweep the debris (real or imagined) from your deck, sidewalk, or driveway.

Group Activities

The following activities are great for a group of siblings or
neighborhood children. They're perfect to do on outings or
camping trips, or at birthday parties and other special celebrations. Some of the games, like "Mother, May I?" and "Line Tag,"
will keep children continually active. Others, like relay races,
will give children periods of rest as they wait for their turns.
Keep the pace of these activities lively to reduce the time that
the children are inactive. You can do many of the activities
indoors as well as out, and many of the races can be run
individually or as relays.

Sardines

This is a fun alternative to a traditional game of hide-and-seek. Choose one child to hide; have the remaining children cover their eyes while he hides. When he's hidden, have the children quietly search for him. As each searcher finds the hider, he or she stays in the hiding place with the hider until all the children have found the hider. Choose a new child to hide and begin the game again.

Line Tag

This game begins like a traditional game of tag, but it has a fun twist!

Choose one child to be It. It chases the other players until he tags one. The tagged player joins hands with It, and the pair continues to chase other players. When the pair tags the next child, he joins them, and so on until all the players have been tagged.

Variation: Whenever the tagged group has four players, split it into two pairs and have the pairs continue chasing untagged players.

Bola

This game is perfect for older preschoolers.

Small, soft rubber ball
Knee-high sock
5-foot-long rope

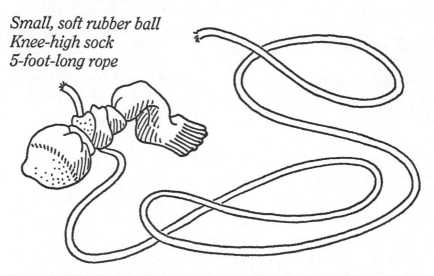

To make a bola, insert the rubber ball into the toe of the sock. Tie a knot in the sock just above the ball, then tie the rope to the sock. Lie on your back and start spinning the bola. When the bola is spinning at a consistent speed (but not too quickly), have the children jump into its path and try to jump over it as it comes around. If you like, have two children join hands and try to jump together.

Mother, May I?

I've modified this version of the classic game to suit very young children.

Chalk or ropes

Use chalk or ropes to make two lines about twenty feet apart on the grass or pavement. Choose one child to be Mother. Have all the children except Mother stand along one line. Mother stands on the other line, facing away from the children. To begin the game, Mother says, "Children, take one giant step" or "Children, take two baby steps" or "Children, take two bunny steps (hops)." Before the children can move, they must ask, "Mother, may I?" Mother can answer yes or no. If the children forget to ask, "Mother, may I?" or if they move after Mother says no, they must return to the start line. When the children reach Mother, choose another child to be Mother and begin again. If you like, have the children take different kinds of steps to reach Mother: regular steps, scissors steps (one foot placed in front and one foot behind, then jumping up and switching the back foot to the front position and the front foot to the back position, while moving forward), or banana steps (lying stretched out on the ground, keeping the feet on the same spot where they'd stood, marking where the head is, then standing there).

Variation: Have each child in line ask, "Mother, may I take five giant steps (or two baby steps, or three bunny steps)?" Mother answers yes or no. Have each child ask until one reaches Mother and becomes the new Mother.

In and Out My Window

This is a modified version of the game Duck, Duck, Goose.

Have the children stand in a circle, arms' width apart from one another, and hold hands. Choose one child to start the game and have him walk around the outside of the circle. After a while, he chooses an opponent to race against by tapping that player on the shoulder. To begin the race, have all the other children in the circle raise their arms. Starting from the same place, the two players must run in opposite directions, weaving in and out of the spaces between the children. The first child to reach the empty spot joins the circle, while the other child walks around the outside of the circle and chooses another player to race.

Soccer Fun

Soccer ball

Divide the children equally into two teams. Have the teams stand about six feet apart in two rows facing each other. Give a soccer ball to one of the children and have him kick it to the child directly opposite him. That player then kicks it back to the second child in the opposite line, who kicks it to the child directly opposite him, and so on until the ball reaches the last child in line. The last child picks up the ball and runs to the other end of his line and kicks it to the first child in the opposite line. Play continues until all the children are in their original positions or until they tire of the game.

Variation: Have the teammates stand one behind another. Have the first children in line face each other. Give the ball to one of the first children in line. To play, each child kicks the ball to the player facing him, then runs to the back of the line after kicking the ball. Continue playing until all the children have had a turn kicking the ball or until they tire of the game.

Feather Race

Ropes or chalk
Paper plate
Craft feathers

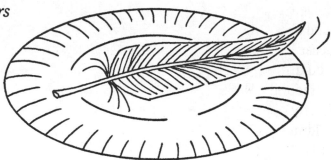

Use ropes or chalk to mark a start line and a finish line about ten to fifteen feet apart on the grass or pavement. Have each child stand at the start line, hold a paper plate in one hand, and keep his other hand behind his back. Place a craft feather on each plate. At your signal, have the children walk as quickly as they can to the finish line. If a feather blows off a plate, that player must return to the start line for another feather (or if you like, simply have him pick up the feather, replace it on the plate, and continue the race). The first player to cross the finish line with a feather on his plate wins.

Variation: Divide the children equally into two or more teams and make it a relay race.

Little Brown Bear

Chalk, paint, or ropes

Use chalk, paint, or ropes to make two lines fifteen to twenty feet apart on the grass or pavement. Choose one child to be Little Brown Bear. Have Little Brown Bear stand between the lines while the other children stand along one line facing him. Little Brown Bear calls, "Who's afraid of the little brown bear?" The children answer, "Not me!" Little Brown Bear responds, "Then you must all skip (or hop, run, gallop) to the other side!" As the children race to get behind the other line, Little Brown Bear tries to tag as many children as possible. Tagged players stay between the lines and help Little Brown Bear catch the untagged players during the next round of play. Continue to play until all the children have been caught, then choose another Little Brown Bear and play again.

Dodge Ball

This is a fun game for four or more children.

Large, soft ball (or crumpled-up newspaper bound with tape, or onion-bag netting stuffed with cotton balls or batting)

Have the children form a circle. Choose one child to stand in the middle, then play the game in one or more of the following ways:
- Each player in the circle takes a turn throwing the ball at the child in the middle, who tries to dodge out of the way. When the child in the middle gets hit, he changes places with the child who hit him.
- Have the children in the circle kick rather than throw the ball toward the child in the middle.
- Have the children in the circle join hands. Give the ball to the child in the middle and have him throw or kick it toward the circle. When a child gets hit, he changes places with the child who hit him.

Crab Race

Ropes or chalk
Chairs (optional)
Balloons, 1 per player (optional)

Use ropes or chalk to mark a start line and a finish line ten to fifteen feet apart on the grass or pavement. Have each child lean back and ease his hands to the ground so they're in line with his shoulders, then raise his bottom off the ground. At your signal, have the children crab-walk to the finish line.

Variations:
- Extend the race by setting up a row of chairs instead of marking a finish line. Players crab-walk around a chair and back to the start line to end the race.

- Divide the children equally into teams and have a crab-walk relay.
- For older children, have them try crab-walking with a balloon on each of their tummies.

Caution: Balloon pieces can pose an extreme choking hazard for very young children, so any balloon play must be carefully supervised.

Keep Away

You can play this game with as few as three players.

Large, soft ball

Choose one player to be It. Have the other players stand in a circle around It. Give one player a ball and have him try to throw it to another player on the other side of the circle. It must try to intercept the ball. If he's successful, he changes places with the player who threw the ball. If he has trouble intercepting the ball, make a rule that the ball must bounce once before It or the other players can catch the ball.

Variation: Have the players pass the ball in other ways, like kicking, rolling, and so on.

Pretzel Race

This race is best for older preschoolers. It can be difficult for toddlers.

Ropes or chalk

Use ropes or chalk to mark a start line and a finish line about ten feet apart on the grass or pavement. Have the children line up along the start line. At your signal, have each child lift one leg and wrap it around the other leg, cross his arms in front of his body, and hop to the finish line.

Sandwich Race

Ropes or chalk
1 ball for each pair of players

Use rope or chalk to mark a start line and a finish line on the grass or pavement. Have the children form pairs and have each pair sit back to back at the start line. Place a ball between the backs of each pair. Have the children link arms and stand. At your signal, the pairs race to the finish line while keeping the ball between their backs. If the ball drops, the pair must return to the start line and begin again. The first pair to cross the finish line without dropping their ball wins.

Circle Ball

Soccer or other playground ball

Have the children form a circle. Make sure each child's legs are twelve to eighteen inches apart and each foot touches the foot of the player next to him. Once the game begins, the children may not move their feet.

   Give one child a ball and have him try to throw or roll the ball between the legs of another player. The children must try to keep the ball from passing between their legs by bending at the waist and using their hands to knock the ball away toward another player. If the ball passes between a player's legs, that child is out but remains in the circle. He must fold his arms in front of him or place his hands on his head; he can no longer try to stop the ball from passing between his legs. Return the ball to the circle and have the remaining players try to knock the ball between the legs of other players until there's only one player left in the game.

Variations:
- If you like, have players place one hand on their heads the first time the ball goes between their legs and let them continue playing until the ball goes between their legs a second time.
- When a player knocks the ball between the legs of someone who's out, that player is also out.

Horsy

Chalk, paint, or ropes

Use chalk, paint, or ropes to make two lines about twenty feet apart on the grass or pavement. Choose one child to be Horsy. Have Horsy stand between the two lines, while the other children stand on one line facing him. The children call out, "Horsy, Horsy, will you take us for a ride?" Horsy responds, "Only if you are wearing red (green, blue, pink, and so on)." Those children wearing the named color may run safely to the other line, while the others must try to cross the line before Horsy tags them. Tagged players stay between the lines and help Horsy catch players during the next round of play. Continue to play until everyone has been tagged, then choose another Horsy and play again.

Relay Tag

Ball, beanbag, or other small object

Choose one child to be It. Give another child a ball. At your signal, It tries to tag the player carrying the ball. This player can hand off the ball to another player to avoid being tagged. It must continue to chase the player holding the ball until he tags him. The tagged player becomes It. Continue until all the children have been It, or until they tire of the game.

Chain Race

Ropes or chalk

Use ropes or chalk to mark a start line and a finish line on the grass or pavement. Have the children form pairs and line up along the start line. Have each pair link arms. At your signal, have the pairs race to the finish line.

Variation: Divide the children equally into two teams. Have all teammates link arms and let the teams race to the finish line.

Shuttle Run

Rope or chalk
Several different small
objects, like Duplo
pieces, blocks, or toy
cars (one of each
object per player)
One basket per player

Use rope or chalk to mark a line on the grass or pavement. Place the baskets along the line and have each child stand beside a basket. Place groups of objects at various distances from the start line; for example, place Duplo pieces four feet from the start line, blocks six feet from the start line, and toy cars eight feet from the start line. At your signal, have each child run to the closest group of objects, pick one up, run and place it in his basket, run to the next group of objects, pick one up, run and place it in his basket, and so on, until he has picked up one of each object. Have each child sit after he's placed the last object in his basket. The first child to sit wins.

Variation: Have the children hop, crawl, tiptoe, and so on instead of run.

Soccer Red Light, Green Light

Rope or chalk
Soccer balls, 1 for each player

Use rope or chalk to mark a start line on the grass or pavement. Have the children stand on the line with their soccer balls on the ground in front of them. Choose one child to be the traffic light and have him stand facing away from the other players, about twenty-five feet from the start line. When the traffic light says, "Green light!" all the players push theirs balls with their feet (dribble) toward him. When he says, "Red light!" and turns around, all the players must freeze. If the traffic light sees anyone moving, the caught players must go back to the start line. Play resumes when the traffic light says, "Green light!" and continues until one of the players reaches him. That player becomes the traffic light, and the game begins again.

Variation: Have each child throw a beanbag, roll a ball, or toss the lid of an ice-cream pail instead of dribbling a soccer ball.

Inside, Outside

Rope or chalk
Several beanbags, paper balls, rolled-up socks,
  or other soft objects

Use a rope or chalk to form a large circle (at least five feet in diameter) on the grass or pavement. Place the beanbags inside the circle. Choose one player to stand inside the circle, while the other players stand several feet outside the circle. At your signal, the player inside the circle begins to throw all the objects outside the circle. The other players try to catch them and throw them back into the circle. Continue play for a minute or two. When time's up, count the number of objects inside the circle and outside. If there are more objects outside the circle than inside, choose a new player to stand inside the circle. If not, the same player remains and tries again to keep as many objects outside the circle as possible.

Variations:
- For a large group of children, make a larger circle and have more than one player standing inside the circle.
- Make a rule that the players outside the circle must stay in one place to catch the objects.

Run the Gauntlet

Ropes or chalk
1 or 2 soft balls

Use ropes or chalk to form two lines, fifteen to twenty feet apart, on the grass or pavement. Choose one or two players and give these players each a ball. Have one chosen player stand midway between the lines at one end. If you've chosen two players, have the second player stand midway between the lines at the other end. Have the remaining children stand along one of the lines. At your signal, the children must run from one line to the other while the chosen players throw their balls and try to hit one of the runners. If a child is hit by a ball, he must change places with the player who threw it. While the throwers retrieve their balls, have the children form another line and prepare to run again.

Cat Tail Tag

2-foot lengths of yarn or string

Tuck yarn or string securely into the waistband of each player to make a tail. To begin the game, players chase one another, trying to pull out tails. When a player pulls out a tail, he gives the tail to its owner and continues to chase the others. Players whose tails have been pulled out must sit. The last player with his tail in place wins.

Variation: Have players hold on to the tails they pull out; players whose tails have been pulled out must sit. When there's one player left with his tail in place, the player who has collected the most tails wins.

Cat and Mouse

Divide the children equally into two teams. One team are cats; the other, mice. Have the cats stand side by side and turn their backs to the mice. Have the mice stand side by side some distance away from the cats and quietly creep up behind them. When the mice are a few feet from the cats, you shout, "The mice are coming!" The cats turn and run after the mice, tagging as many as they can. Tagged mice join the cats. The mice now turn their backs to the cats, who now creep up on the mice. When the cats are a few feet from the mice, you shout, "The cats are coming!" The mice tag as many cats as they can. Continue to play until all the children are cats or mice, or until they tire of the game.

Stones

Ropes or chalk

Use ropes or chalk to mark two lines at least twenty feet apart on the grass or pavement. Choose one child to be the stone. The stone sits midway between the two lines, and the other players skip around him while staying in between the lines. When the stone jumps up, the players must run to the other side of either line before the stone tags them. Any player tagged by the stone also becomes a stone and must sit between the lines. The remaining players continue to skip around the stones, but no tagged stone can move or chase players until the first stone moves. The game continues until all the children have been turned into stones. The last child to become a stone begins the next round as the first stone.

Sharks and Minnows

Ropes or chalk

Use ropes or chalk to mark two lines about twenty feet apart on the grass or pavement. Choose one child to be Mr. Shark and have him stand between the two lines. Have the other children (the minnows) stand on one of the lines. To begin the game, the minnows call to the shark, "Mr. Shark, Mr. Shark, we want to come and swim!" Mr. Shark replies, "Minnow friends, minnow friends, won't you please come in?" All the minnows then run to the other line while Mr. Shark tries to tag as many minnows as possible. Tagged minnows become seaweed and sit between the lines with Mr. Shark for the next round; they can't chase the other minnows, but they can tag them as they run by. Play continues until all the minnows have been turned into seaweed. The last player to be tagged becomes Mr. Shark.

Throwing Race

Ropes or chalk
Balls or beanbags, 1 for each player

Use ropes or chalk to mark a start line and a finish line on the grass or pavement. Have the children stand on the start line with their balls or beanbags in their hands. At your signal, have the children throw their balls as far as they can, run to pick them up, and throw them again, repeating this process until they reach the finish line. The first player to cross the finish line wins.

Variation: Have children roll or kick their balls or beanbags, or push them along with their noses.

Sock Tag

4 pairs of rolled-up socks

Choose two players to be Its and give each of these players two pairs of rolled-up socks. Have the other players run around while the Its try to hit them with the socks. Tagged players must sit, and the game ends when all players are sitting. Choose two new players to be Its and begin the game again.

Variation: A tagged player may grab a pair of socks, if they're within reach, and throw them. If he tags another player, he rejoins the game and the tagged player sits. If he tags an It, he becomes an It.

Block the Ball

As few as four players can play this fun game.

Empty plastic soda bottles, plastic bowling pins, paper towel rolls, or other objects that can be easily knocked over Several balls or beanbags

Divide players equally into two teams and have each team set up a row of soda bottles. Make sure the rows are parallel to each other and are spaced about fifteen feet apart. Have each team stand in front of its row, with teammates standing side by side. Give each team several balls or beanbags. Each team takes a turn rolling a ball or throwing a beanbag to try and knock over the other team's bottles. Teams try to protect their bottles by blocking the balls or catching the beanbags. The first team to knock over all of the other team's bottles wins.

Veggie Relay

Hula-Hoop or rope
Several carrots, potatoes,
* or other garden vegetables*
* (or beanbags, balls, or*
* other small objects)*
Buckets or baskets,
* 1 for each team*

Set the Hula-Hoop on the ground or make a large circle on the
ground with the rope. Place the vegetables inside the circle.
Divide the children equally into teams. Have the teams stand
an equal distance from the circle and an equal distance from
one another. Have teammates line up behind one another, and
place a basket at the end of each line.

At your signal, the first child in each team runs to the circle,
picks up a vegetable, runs back to his team, and tags the hand
of the next player in line. That player runs to pick up a vegetable
while the first player goes to the back of the line and places
his vegetable into the basket. Play continues with each player
retrieving a vegetable and placing it in his team's basket until
all the vegetables are gone from the circle. The team with the
most vegetables in its basket wins.

Chapter 3

Indoor Activities

What children take from us, they give...
We become people who feel more deeply, question
more deeply, hurt more deeply, and love more deeply.

—Sonia Taitz

Parenting active children can seem easy during sunny summer days. Kids can burn up their seemingly never-ending energy in the fresh, warm air. But after a week of rain or subzero temperatures, keeping kids busy indoors can test a parent's patience! Days like these can seem to last forever, and you may be tempted to occupy your child's time with TV or computer games. Sedentary activities like watching TV and playing computer games aren't harmful when the time spent doing them is short and infrequent, but they can harm your child's physical and mental health if they make up most of her day's activities. Young children need to spend most of every day moving and using their imaginations, rain or shine!

Although there will be days when you and your child are confined inside, that doesn't mean you can't be active. Put on some snappy music and have an exercise class in your living room, play "Follow the Leader" around the house, make up a dance, invite friends over and organize active games for the kids to play indoors—the possibilities are endless! The important lesson is to include activities in your child's daily routine that will get her moving, and the activities in this chapter will help you do just that.

Locomotor Activities

The activities in this section will keep your child busy in your home while helping her develop locomotor skills like walking, running, hopping, skipping, and more.

Hoops

Several Hula-Hoops
Action Cube (optional; see Appendix)
Recording of music (optional)

Lay the Hula-Hoops on the floor in a row so they touch one another. Choose a way for your child to move (jumping, hopping, skipping, and so on) and have her move that way from hoop to hoop. If you like, roll the Action Cube to select a movement.

Variation: Play some music and have your child move to the beat from hoop to hoop.

Footprints

Marker
Paper
Scissors
Tape

Trace several adult-size footprints (left and right) on the paper, then cut them out and tape them to the floor in curvy or loopy paths. Have your child follow the footprints by placing her feet only on the footprints.

Paper Mountain

Newspaper or other scrap paper
Empty wading pool (optional)

Have your child crumple up sheets of newspaper one at a time
and throw them into an empty wading pool or designated area.
Let her keep adding paper until she creates a paper mountain.
Have her explore inside the mountain, climb over it, roll on it,
jump on it, run through it, or whatever she wishes to do.
When she's done, recycle the newspaper.

Basket of Balls

Several medium-size balls
Large basket
Stopwatch, hourglass, or recording of a song (optional)
6 to 12 tennis or Ping-Pong balls and muffin pan (optional)

Dump the balls on the floor and have your child race to put all
the balls into the basket. If you like, time how long it takes her
to complete the task or have her try to collect the balls before
an hourglass runs out or a song finishes playing.

Variation: Use tennis or Ping-Pong balls and have your child
race to put each into a section of a muffin pan.

Shoebox Walking

Hole punch or letter opener
2 shoeboxes
Two 3-foot lengths of yarn or string
Recording of "Skater's Waltz" (optional)

Punch a small hole in the center of each long side of the shoe-boxes. For each shoebox, thread the yarn or string through the holes and tie the ends together to make a big loop. Have your child place one foot into each shoebox and hold onto the strings. Have her try walking, running, or dancing in her giant feet.

Variation: Play a recording of "Skater's Waltz" as she pretends to skate on a carpeted floor.

Maze

Chairs

Place chairs so they make a maze around the room. Your child will enjoy moving through the maze in the following ways:

- Crawl under the chairs.
- Crawl around the chairs, weaving from the back of one chair to the front of the next.

Set the chairs next to one another as you make the maze, then spot your child as she moves through it in the following ways:

- Crawl along the seats of the chairs.
- Walk along the seats of the chairs.

Sticky Feet Marching

2-foot length of clear contact paper
Tape
Recording of music (optional)

Remove the backing of the contact paper and tape it, sticky side up, to the floor. Have your child march in place with bare feet on the paper; she'll enjoy the sticky sensation and sound. If you like, play some music and have her hop, jump, and dance on the paper.

Circle Hop

Scissors
2-yard length of yarn
1-yard length of yarn

On the floor, form a circle with the longer length of yarn. Inside that circle, form another circle with the shorter length of yarn. Have your child try the following moves:

- Hop inside each circle and out again. Change feet and repeat.
- Jump with both feet together into the large circle then the small circle. Turn around and jump out again.
- Jump from outside the large circle and land in the small circle. Turn around and jump out again without touching the inside of the larger circle.
- Jump or hop with closed eyes until she thinks she's inside the smaller circle.

Variation: Add circles made from three-, four-, and five-yard lengths of yarn.

Toehold Walk

Have your child bend at the waist and grab her toes or ankles.
Have her try to walk forward, backward, and sideways while in
this position.

Variation: Have her cross her hands before grabbing her toes
so her right hand holds her left toes and her left hand holds
her right toes.

Mountain Climbing

Couch cushions or large pillows
Step stool (optional)
Bed mattress (optional)

- Make a big pile of couch cushions or large pillows on the floor. Be sure the pile is well away from any table legs or hard edges. Let your child climb and roll around on the pile.
- Stack the cushions like stairs against a couch, coffee table, or bed and let her practice climbing up and down.
- Hold your toddler's hand as she practices climbing up and down a step stool or set of stairs.
- Place one end of a bed mattress on the floor, the other end on a bed or couch. Have your child climb up the mattress and down again.

Dice Action

Use dice in combination with an Action Cube to come up with a number of movement possibilities!

Action Cube (see Appendix)
Pair of dice

Have your child roll the Action Cube to determine what movement she'll use (for example, *jump*). Roll the dice (use only one die for very young children). Have your child count the dots on the dice to determine the number of times she'll do the movement. Have her roll the Action Cube and dice again to do a new set of movements.

Wheelbarrow

Have your child lie on her tummy on the floor. Stand behind her at her feet, grab her ankles, and lift them up. Your child must use only her hands or forearms to move herself around the room. If there are two or more children, have them try this activity with one another.

Variation: Grab your child's knees instead of her ankles.

Balloon Walk

Small balloon
Beanbag or pillow (optional)

Inflate the balloon and place it between your child's knees. Have her practice walking forward and backward without dropping the balloon. How fast can she walk without dropping the balloon? Can she jump in place and forward and backward without dropping the balloon?

Variation: Use a beanbag or pillow instead of a balloon.

Caution: Balloon pieces can pose an extreme choking hazard for very young children, so any balloon play must be carefully supervised.

Indoor Obstacle Course

An obstacle course is a fun way to get some exercise on a rainy, house-bound day! A toddler will need only four or five stations; older preschoolers can manage up to ten. Many ideas in this book, including those that follow, make great obstacle course stations:

- Jump into a pile of pillows.
- Hop around plush animals set in a zigzag path.
- Walk on hands and feet between the rungs of a ladder laid on the floor.
- Do a somersault on a mat.
- Jump off a step stool.
- Run up and down a short flight of stairs.

Paper Plate Pull

Hole punch or sharp pencil
Paper plate
2- or 3-foot length of yarn or string
Small objects in different sizes and weights

Poke a hole near the edge of the paper plate. Thread the yarn or string through the hole and tie the ends together. Have your child hold the string and pull the plate. Place a small object on the plate and have your child try pulling the plate around without the object falling off. Try adding objects. See if your child can choose objects to pull that won't fall off.

Side Glides

Show your child how to do side glides, which are like sideways gallops. Starting with your hands on your hips and legs shoulders' width apart, move your right foot to the right, then quickly move your left foot to meet the right. As soon as the left foot meets the right, move the right foot to the right again and have the left foot follow. Side glide in a large circle, across the room, or on a zigzag path. Speed up and slow down. Change direction by starting with the left leg and having the right foot follow.

Walk Tall

Show your child how to walk with good posture (shoulders down and back, stomach in, neck lengthened, and chin level). Have her copy your movements: Walk faster and slower. Walk in place, lifting your knees as high as possible. Walk backward and on tiptoe (these moves may be difficult for young toddlers).

Variation: Repeat this activity with running, hopping, skipping, and other locomotor movements your child can do.

Blanket Scoot

Baby blanket or towel

Lay the baby blanket or towel on a smooth floor. Have your child sit on the blanket or towel with her bare feet sticking out beyond the edge. Have her use only her feet to propel herself across the floor. Can she move backward? Have her turn in circles. Have her place her knees next to her chest, her feet against a wall, and push off. How far can she go?

Body Parts

This is a good activity to help toddlers learn to identify parts of their bodies. Say to your child, "Touch your head, touch your tummy, touch your toes." Demonstrate the actions as you give the instructions. After she does the actions, repeat the instructions, reversing or mixing up the order in which you say them. Go faster and slower. Ask your child to touch less familiar body parts like her heel, hip, spine, elbow, wrist, and ankle.

Hoop Play

Hula-Hoop

Lay the hoop on the floor and ask your child to do the following:
- Jump in and out of the hoop.
- Walk, skip, march, and hop around the outside of the hoop.
- Stand inside the hoop, then march, hop, and jump in place.
- Pick up the hoop and roll it along the floor.

Fishing

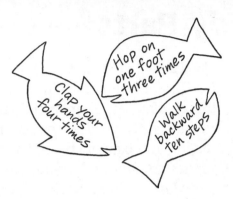

Scissors
Construction paper
Marker
Tape
Paper clips
Magnet
String

Cut fish shapes from construction paper. On each fish, write an instruction like "Hop three times," "Walk backward ten steps," "Balance on one foot and count to three," "Clap your hands four times," "Jump with feet together five times," and so on. On the back of each fish, tape a paper clip. Place the fish, paper clip side up, on the floor. Tie a magnet to the string. Have your child dangle the magnet over the fish. When she catches one, she must reel it in and perform the action written on the fish.

Green Light, Red Light

Scissors and red and green construction paper (optional)

Stand twenty to twenty-five feet away from your child. When you say, "Green light," have her walk, run, hop, skip, or crawl toward you. Have her move in a variety of ways: forward, backward, sideways, slowly, quickly, straight, curved, zigzag, and so on. She must stop when you say, "Red light."

Variation: Cut out a circle from red construction paper and another from green. Have your child move when you hold up the green circle and stop when you hold up the red.

Box Tunnel

Scissors
3 or more large cardboard boxes (each roughly the same
    size and big enough for your child to crawl through)
Packing tape

Remove the top and bottom flaps of each box, then tape the boxes together to form a tunnel. Your child will have fun crawling through and around the tunnel.

Can You?

Ask your toddler what she can do: "Can you nod your head? Can you clap your hands? Can you stamp your feet? Can you rub your tummy? Can you raise one arm? Can you touch your nose? Can you put your hand on your foot? Can you touch your elbow with your hand?" Have her do the actions to prove she can.

Copycat

Beanbag
Scissors
Magazines
Glue
Several sheets of construction paper

Cut pictures from magazines that show various actions like running, jumping, standing on one foot, crawling, and so on. Glue the pictures onto separate sheets of construction paper and place them face-down on the floor. Have your child throw a beanbag so it lands on or near one of the sheets. Have her turn the paper over and perform the action shown.

Stability Activities

Turning, twisting, bending, stopping, rolling, jumping, landing, and other balance skills are easy to practice indoors. You don't need a lot of open space or large props. When trying the following stability activities with your child, be sure to follow a logical progression. Use a wide, stable base of support before letting your child try a narrower or unstable one. Have your child master balancing at low heights before she attempts higher heights. Follow your child closely so you're ready to steady her if she wavers. Finally, be sure she can balance herself before adding objects like beanbags to the activity.

Sitting Balance

Have your child sit on the floor and grab her toes. Have her straighten her legs and lift them, then lean back so her body forms a V. Tell her to slowly let go of her toes while keeping her legs lifted, then hold her arms straight to the sides to maintain her balance. How long can she stay in this position?

Arm Balance

Have your child sit on the floor with her legs straight in front of her. Have her place one hand on the floor beside and slightly behind her, then turn and raise her body to that side, keeping it straight, so her arm supports the weight of her body. Repeat with the other arm.

Crisscross

Beanbag (optional)

Have your child stand with her arms folded across her chest.
Have her cross one leg over the other. Can she sit then get up
in this position without losing her balance? Can she do it
while balancing a beanbag on her head?

Symmetry

Symmetry is when the sides of an object or shape are mirror
images of each other. Make one side of your body a mirror
image of the other. Have your child copy your movements. For
example, raise both arms, move both thumbs, open and close
both fists, bend both elbows. Place your hands on your shoulders, then on your knees, then on your toes. Hold both arms
out to the side, then straight in front of you. Bend at the waist
and touch your toes. Do any other symmetrical movements
you can think of. Let your child make symmetrical
movements and follow her lead.

Balance Challenge

Beanbag or paper plate (optional)

- Have your child stand with arms stretched out to the sides. Have her slowly lift one leg and balance for five seconds. Repeat with the other leg.
- If you like, set a beanbag or paper plate on your child's head. With her arms stretched out to the sides and balancing on one foot, have her slowly fold her arms across her chest, then stretch them out again. Can she keep the beanbag or plate on her head while she does this? Repeat with the other leg.
- Have your child stand with arms stretched out to the sides. Tell her to slowly extend one leg behind her body. How long can she hold the position? Repeat with the other leg.
- If you like, set a beanbag or paper plate on your child's head. With her arms stretched out to the sides and one leg extended behind her, have her fold her arms across her chest then stretch them out again. Can she keep the beanbag or plate on her head while she does this? Repeat with the other leg.

Ball Balancing

Large playground or exercise ball

Have your child lie across the ball on her stomach. Hold onto her hands or feet and help her balance on the ball. Can she balance when you let go? Grab her hands or feet again and pull her forward and push her back. Have your child try rolling on her own by pushing off with her hands, stopping herself, then pushing off with her feet.

Balance Blocks

At least six wooden blocks
Beanbag (optional)

Set the blocks on the floor so they're a child's step away from one another. Have your child try to step from block to block without losing her balance. Can she balance a beanbag on her head as she goes?

Body Bowling

Plastic bowling pins or empty plastic soda bottles

Set the pins or soda bottles so they form a large circle. Have your child lie down in the center of the circle and roll outward to topple the pins. If you like, set the pins in a row and have your child roll toward them.

Body Letters

Marker
Index cards
Alphabet cards (optional)

Write the following letters separately on index cards: *C, I, D, L, O, P, S, U,* and *V.* Hold up a card and have your child make the shape with her body. Make cards for the letters *A, T, X,* and *Y,* then work with your child or have your child work with a partner to form these letters.

Variation: If you like, use a set of alphabet cards. Have your child make the letters she can form on her own, then try those she can make with a partner. Have her tell you which letters she can't make alone or with a partner.

Stork Stand

Beanbag (optional)

Have your child stand with both feet together and arms stretched out to the sides. Tell her to shift all her weight to her left leg, then raise her right foot so the sole rests against the inside of her left knee and thigh. Have her hold this position for a moment or two before returning her right foot to the floor. Have her repeat the movement with her left foot. If you like, place a beanbag on her head. Can she do the movement without dropping the beanbag?

Variation: Have your child repeat the movement with her arms folded across her chest.

Beanbag Balance

Beanbag or paper plate
Masking tape

Have your child use a beanbag or paper plate to practice keeping her balance in the following ways:
- Place a beanbag on her head. How far can she walk before the beanbag falls off? Have her speed up and slow down.
- Place a beanbag on her head, then have her climb a flight of stairs. Can she get to the top without the beanbag falling off?
- How far can she walk with a beanbag on her outstretched palm? Have her walk slowly and quickly.
- Have her get on her hands and knees. Place a beanbag on her back and have her crawl around the room slowly and quickly. Can she keep the beanbag on her back? Place the beanbag on her head. How far can she crawl before it falls off?
- Use masking tape to make a curved or zigzag path on the floor. Can your child walk on the tape while balancing a beanbag on her head?

Leg Cross

Have your child stand with arms stretched out to the sides. Keeping her left foot on the ground, have her cross her right leg over the left so her right foot points down and her big toe touches the ground. Have her try to return to the starting position without losing her balance or wavering. Repeat with the left leg.

Variation: Have your child repeat the movement with her arms folded across her chest.

Knee Lift Balance

Beanbag (optional)

Have your child stand with both feet together and arms stretched out to the sides. Have her lift her right knee so her thigh is parallel to the ground and her right toes are pointed down. If you like, place a beanbag on her thigh. How long can she balance it there? Repeat with the left leg.

Variation: Have your child repeat the movement with her arms folded across her chest.

Rocking

- Have your child lie on her stomach on the floor. Show her how to raise her head and feet and grab her ankles. How long can she rock like a rocking horse?
- Have your child lie on her back on the floor. Tell her to bring her knees to her chest, wrap her arms around her knees, then rock back and forth.

Candlestick Jump

Short unlit candlestick

Set the candlestick on the floor in front of your child. Have her stand with feet together in front of the candlestick and recite the familiar nursery rhyme together.

Jack be nimble, Jack be quick,
Jack jump over the candlestick!

On the word *candlestick*, have her bend her knees, swing her arms, and jump over the candlestick, landing on both feet.

Tiptoe Balance

Standing on tiptoe is an important stability skill and is difficult for some children to master. Have your child stand on tiptoe as long as possible. Together count out loud the seconds she can stay on tiptoe. If you like, have her walk forward and backward on tiptoe.

Toddler Trampoline

Crib mattress, bed mattress, or thick foam padding
Sheet or blanket
Pillows

Place a mattress or foam padding on the floor, away from any sharp edges or corners. Cover it with a sheet or blanket and surround it with pillows. Have your toddler try one or more of the following activities on her mini-trampoline:
- Jump in place.
- Run in place.
- Do a somersault.
- Fall backward.
- Roll from side to side.

Balance Beam

Board about 8 inches wide by 6 feet long
Beanbags
Several books, large blocks of wood, stool, or chair

- Lay the board on the floor. Have your child practice keeping her balance by walking on it. Have her stretch her arms out to the sides and walk back and forth on the board. How fast can she walk? Can she walk backward? Can she balance a beanbag on her head as she walks on the board? Can she balance beanbags on top of her outstretched hands as she walks on the board?
- Raise the board by putting several books or large blocks of wood under each end. Have your child walk along the board in the above ways.
- Place one end of the board on the floor and another on a stack of books or blocks or on a stool or chair. Have your child walk up and down the board in the above ways.

Sponge Shoes

Two 3-foot lengths of yarn or string
2 large rectangular sponges or blocks of foam
Large sheet of paper (optional)
Paint in a low, wide container (optional)
2 empty coffee cans (optional)
Hammer and nail (optional)

Lay one length of yarn or string on the floor and place a sponge on it at the midpoint. Place your child's foot on the sponge. Tie the ends of the yarn together tightly across the top of her foot. Repeat this process for the other foot, then let your child walk on her sponge shoes around your home.

If you like, take this activity outdoors. Lay a large sheet of paper on level ground. Hold your child's hands as she steps into paint then walks on the paper to make sponge prints.

Variation: Use a hammer and nail to punch two holes directly opposite from each other in the sides of a coffee can. Thread the yarn through the holes, then tie the ends of yarn together. Do the same for the other coffee can. Turn the cans upside down and have your child hold onto the yarn and walk on her coffee can stilts.

Skateboard Balance

Skateboard
Beanbag (optional)

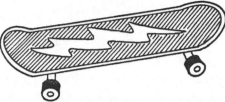

Have your child stand on a
skateboard with her arms
stretched out to the sides. If you like, have her balance a
beanbag on her head as she tries the following moves:

- With her arms stretched out to the sides, have her slowly lift
  one leg and balance for five seconds. Have her repeat this
  movement, but tell her to also slowly fold her arms across
  her chest, then stretch them out again. Have her repeat
  these movements with the other leg.

- With her arms stretched out to the sides, have her slowly
  extend one leg behind her. Can she fold her arms across
  her chest then stretch them out again without losing her
  balance or dropping the beanbag? Have her repeat these
  movements with the other leg.

- With both feet together and her arms stretched out to the
  sides, have her lift her right knee so her thigh is parallel to
  the ground and her right toes are pointed down. Can she
  balance a beanbag on her thigh? Can she fold her arms across
  her chest then stretch them out again without dropping the
  beanbag? Have her repeat these movements for the left leg.

Jumping Up

String or rope
Beach ball, foam ball, or ball made from crumpled newspaper

Use the string or rope to hang the ball from the ceiling. (If using a newspaper ball, leave a corner of the paper sticking out and tie the rope or string around it.) Have your child jump up and bump the ball with her head, hand, shoulder, elbow, and other parts of her body.

Jumping Down

Hula-Hoop, masking tape, or string
Sturdy stool or chair

Place the Hula-Hoop on the floor (or use masking tape or string to make a circle) in front of the stool. Have your child stand on the stool and jump into the circle, landing on both feet. Be prepared to catch or steady your child as she lands.

Rope Jumping

Rope or jump rope
Table, chair, or other sturdy object
Hula-Hoop or masking tape

- Lay the rope or jump rope on the floor and have your child jump over it. Tie one end of the rope to a table or chair leg, hold on to the other end, and have your child jump over the rope. Gradually raise the rope until your child can no longer easily jump over it.
- Tie one end of a rope to a chair leg and tie the other end to the leg of another chair. Pull the chairs apart so the rope is taut. (Or have two people hold the rope.) Have your child jump over the rope and land on both feet inside a Hula-Hoop or an area marked by masking tape.
- Once your child has mastered jumping over a rope, tie one end of the rope to a door handle and gently swing the other end back and forth. Encourage your child to jump over the rope as it moves toward her.

High Jumping

Chalk
String (optional)

Have your child stand in front of a wall with a piece of chalk in her hand. Have her raise her arm and jump as high as she can, touching the chalk to the wall to mark how high she can jump. Have her jump again to see if she can jump higher. If you like, measure the height with string. Save the string to compare with jumps on another day.

Jumping Jacks

Timer

Show your child how to do a jumping jack: Jump up then land with feet wide apart, then jump up again and land with feet together. If you like, clap your hands above your head when your feet land apart and return your arms to your sides when your feet land together. How many jumping jacks can your child do in one minute? How about five minutes?

Swinging

Having your child swing various parts of her body helps develop her stability skills. Do the following movements with her:

- Swing your arms back and forth and from side to side. Swing them slowly and quickly.
- Swing first one leg then the other. Swing them slowly, quickly, and forward and back.
- Bend at the waist and swing your upper body from side to side, slowly and quickly.
- Bend at the waist and swing your arms back and forth in front of you.

Sitting Down

Have your child try the following ways to sit on the ground, starting from a standing position:

- Sit down using her hands.
- Sit down without using her hands.
- Sit down as slowly as possible.
- Sit down quickly with a thump.

Have her repeat the above movements, starting from a kneeling position.

Mirror Gymnastics

Large mirror
Recording of music

Stand with your
child in front of
a large mirror and
do one or more
of the following
actions:

- Encourage her to
  make movements
  like turning, bend-
  ing, twisting, hopping, balancing on one foot, and so on,
  and watch what happens to her reflection as she does.
- Have her face away from the mirror, stand with her feet
  apart, touch her toes, and look between her legs to see her
  upside-down reflection.
- Put on some music and encourage her to move to the beat.

Carpet Jumping

Several carpet squares in different colors or patterns

Lay the squares randomly around a carpeted room (carpet squares placed on an uncarpeted floor may slide out from under your child and injure her). Place the squares next to one another so your child can jump easily from one to the next. Have your child try different ways of moving from square to square: jumping, hopping, leaping, and so on. If you like, lay the squares in a pattern, or call out instructions such as "Hop to the blue square," "Jump to the green square," and so on.

Stair Jumping

Have your child practice keeping her balance by jumping from a stair and landing on both feet. Younger children should start on the first step, while older children can move up a step or two. If necessary, hold your child's hands as she jumps.

Toddler Balance

Challenge your toddler to balance in the following ways:
- on hands and knees
- on two hands and one knee, with her free leg stretched out behind her body (repeat for other leg)
- on one hand and one knee, with her free arm raised to the side and free leg stretched out behind her body (repeat for other side)
- on tiptoe
- on one foot (repeat for other foot)
- on both feet, arms outstretched, leaning forward, backward, and to each side

Standing Up

Just as there's more than one way to sit down, there's more than one way to stand up! Have your child try the following:
- Sit cross-legged on the floor and get up without using her hands.
- Sit with her legs stretched out in front of her and get up without using her hands.
- Lie on her tummy and try to stand without using her hands.
- Lie on her back and try to stand as quickly as possible. Have her repeat the movement, trying to stand as slowly as possible.

Frog Handstand

Have your child squat and place her hands on the floor, with her fingers forward and elbows pressed against the inside of her knees. Have her lean forward very slowly until her full weight is on her hands. Can she lift her feet off the floor and balance on her hands? How long can she hold this position?

Teddy Bear Stand

Gym mat, thick towel, or blanket (optional)

Have your child get on her hands and knees on a gym mat. Have her lower the top of her head to the mat and place her hands about shoulders' width apart (elbows pointing back) on the floor by her head. Help her raise her lower body and place her knees on her bent elbows. How long can she balance in this position? Can she do a teddy bear stand without your help? Many of her teddy bear stands may end as somersaults!

Variation: Once she has mastered the teddy bear stand, have her try to slowly raise her legs until she's doing a headstand.

Follow Me

Recording of snappy music (optional)

Practice simple stability skills with your child by having her follow your movements. Roll across the floor, do a somersault (which may not be as easy to do as when you were a child!), balance on one leg, or jump across a rope. You can incorporate many of the stability activities in this section into the game. If you like, put on some snappy music and move to the beat.

Swaying

Swaying is transferring weight from one side of the body to the other in an easy, relaxed motion.

Recording of music
Scarf or streamer

Show your child how to sway from side to side. Toes should remain on the floor, although toddlers will likely lift their feet completely. Try these swaying activities:

- Hold your child's hand and sway back and forth together, slowly and quickly.
- Put on some music and sway together to the beat.
- Give your child a scarf or streamer to hold in one hand and twirl gently as you sway together.

Scissors Jumps

Do scissors jumps with your child. Stand with feet together, then jump up and land with one foot in front of you and one foot behind. Jump again and switch the placement of your feet. Swing your arms back and forth with each jump. If you like, count, "One, two, one, two," or count how many scissors jumps you can do before you both tire out!

Manipulative Activities

Throwing, catching, batting, and other manipulative skills are often the most difficult to do inside the average home. So to prevent damage, be sure to use soft balls, bats, and other objects, and always put dangerous, breakable items well out of harm's way before you do any of these activities with your child.

Caution: Some of the following activities require balloons. Balloon pieces can pose an extreme choking hazard for young children, so any balloon play must be carefully supervised.

Scoop Games

Utility knife
Gallon-size
* plastic jug*
* (a bleach*
* bottle*
* works*
* best)*
Duct tape
Several tennis balls, Ping-Pong balls, and golf balls

Cut the jug into two pieces by inserting the knife just below the bottom of the handle and cutting diagonally down one side to the opposite bottom corner. Cut down the other side in the same way and recycle the bottom piece. Tape the cut edge of the other half to avoid injury. Your child can use the scoop in the following ways:

- Toss the tennis ball into the air and catch it with the scoop.
- Scatter several tennis, Ping-Pong, and golf balls around the room. How quickly can your child scoop them all up without touching them?

Variation: Make a scoop for another child and have the children throw and catch balls with the scoops.

Easy Toss

Yarn, foam ball, or other soft ball
Marker, sheet of paper, and tape (optional)
Ping-Pong ball and empty plastic soda bottle (optional)

Make a ball by winding yarn into a ball shape, or use a foam ball or other soft ball. Have your child practice her throwing skills by throwing the ball at a wall. If you like, draw a target on paper and tape it to the wall. Can your child hit the target with the ball?

Variation: Place a Ping-Pong ball on top of an empty plastic soda bottle. Can your child hit the ball without knocking over the bottle?

Towel Trampoline

Towel
2 or more tennis balls

Have your child hold one end of a towel while you hold the other. Place a tennis ball on the towel and practice tossing and catching it in the towel. How many times can you toss and catch the ball before it bounces on the floor? Can you toss and catch more than one ball at the same time?

Indoor Bowling

Several plastic bowling pins, empty plastic soda bottles,
*   or unopened paper towel rolls*
Large rubber ball
Unopened can of food or beanbag

Line up the bowling pins, soda bottles, or paper towel rolls.
Have your child stand a distance away from the pins, then roll
the ball to knock them over. In what other ways can she knock
over the pins? Have her try rolling an unopened can of food,
throwing a beanbag, or kicking a ball to upend the pins.

Hammer Game

Several ice cubes
Ziploc bag
Sturdy toy hammer

Place the ice cubes in a Ziploc bag. Have your child use the
toy hammer to smash the cubes into crushed ice.

Rolling Fun

Large rubber ball
Chalk, Hula-Hoop, or laundry basket (optional)

Show your child how to roll a ball. Have her hold the ball in her hands, bend her knees and lean forward, place the ball between her feet, then swing her arms forward and upward as she releases the ball. When your child can properly release the ball, try the following activities:

- Roll the ball on various surfaces: carpet, hardwood floor, bedspread, and so on.
- Roll the ball down a flight of stairs. Walk down and retrieve the ball, then try to roll it up the stairs.
- Practice rolling the ball toward a target, like a chalk mark, Hula-Hoop, or laundry basket turned on its side.

Flipping Fun

Sheet or blanket
Several foam balls or crumpled newspaper balls

Lay the sheet on the floor and place the balls on the sheet. Grab the corners of the sheet at one end and have your child grab the corners at the other end. Together, wave the sheet to make the balls flip off. Have your child retrieve the balls, then play again. Take turns retrieving the balls.

Balloon Bat

Balloon
Toy baseball bat or empty gift-wrapping roll
Hot glue gun
Paper plate
Wooden paint stirrer

Inflate the balloon. Your child can practice her manipulative skills and have fun batting the balloon in the following ways:

- Use a closed fist to hit the balloon around the room.
- Use a toy baseball bat to bat the balloon around the room. Or take turns hitting and catching the balloon.
- Glue a paper plate onto a wooden paint stirrer. Use this paddle to bat the balloon around the room.

Sweeping Fun

Tennis balls, golf balls, popcorn kernels,
crumpled newspaper balls,
Duplo pieces, or other small
lightweight objects
Whiskbroom, small push
broom, or toy broom
Large container

Scatter the objects around the room. Give your child the broom and let her have fun sweeping the objects around the room. If you like, have her sweep all the objects into a large container when she tires of this activity.

Toddler Catch

Toddlers usually catch with their arms straight out in front of them, and it's common for them to pull away from the ball as it approaches them. To make your toddler less apprehensive, try using these ball alternatives when playing catch with her.

Onion bag
Cotton batting or cotton balls
Twist tie or elastic band
Large balloon
Popcorn kernels or uncooked rice
Lightweight scarf

- Stuff the onion bag with as much cotton as possible. Close the top of the bag with a twist tie or elastic band. Toss the ball back and forth with your child.
- Place a spoonful of popcorn kernels in a large balloon to give it a little weight. Inflate the balloon and tie the end, then use it to play catch.
- Throw a lightweight scarf to your child; it will move slowly through the air, giving her plenty of time to prepare for the catch.

Dump Truck

2 large containers
Basket or small bucket with handle
Small toys
Child's wagon or doll stroller
Large toy dump truck
Towel, sheet, or baby blanket

Fill one large container with small toys. Place the other container across the room from the full one. Have your child use one or more of the following ways to transfer the toys from the full container to the empty one.

- Have her fill a basket or bucket with toys from the full container, carry them across the room, and dump them into the empty container.
- Have her fill a wagon or doll stroller with toys, wheel it across the room, and dump the toys from the wagon or stroller to the empty container.
- Have her load a toy dump truck with toys, push the truck across the room, and dump the toys into the empty container.
- Spread a towel, sheet, or baby blanket on a smooth floor. Have your child place the small toys on the blanket, pull it across the room, and transfer the toys into the empty container.

Foot Dribble

2 long ropes of equal length
Masking tape
Soccer ball or large rubber ball

Tape the ropes to the floor to make a path. You can make a straight, curved, or zigzag path. Give your child a soccer ball and have her push the ball with her foot (dribble) up and down the path.

Indoor Curling

Masking tape
Hockey puck, Frisbee, plastic lid or plate, unopened can of
*   tuna, or other disk-shaped object*
Toy broom
Stopwatch (optional)

Lay a long line of tape on the floor. If you like, lay the tape in a circular or zigzag pattern. Have your child use the broom to push a hockey puck or other disk-shaped object along the line. If you like, time your child, then have her try to beat her time.

Kicking Practice

Soccer ball or large rubber ball
Chalk, Hula-Hoop, or laundry basket
Stopwatch (optional)

Try the following activities to give your child some kicking practice:
- Stand several feet away from your child. Slowly roll a ball toward her and have her kick it back to you.
- Kick a ball toward your child and have her kick it back to you.
- Have your child kick a ball toward a target, like a chalk mark, Hula-Hoop, or laundry basket turned on its side.
- Designate a goal some distance away from your child. Have her kick the ball, run after it, kick it again, and so on, until she reaches the goal. If you like, time your child and see if she can improve her time.

Indoor Soccer

Toy soccer net or painter's tape
Foam soccer ball

Use a toy soccer net or tape a goal area to the wall. Have your child try to kick the ball into the net while you guard the goal. After a while, let your child be the goalie while you try to kick the ball into the net.

Newspaper Delivery

Several sections of newspaper
Rubber bands
Large box or container
Boxes and containers in various sizes (optional)

Roll up several sections of newspaper and secure them with rubber bands. Have your child throw the newspapers into a large box or container. Vary the distance from which your child throws. In addition to aiming for the box, have her throw near to and far from the box, and in front of and behind the box. If you like, use several containers in various sizes and have her try to throw the newspapers into them.

Do This, Do That

This game is similar to Simon Says. You be the leader. Your child copies your actions whenever you say, "Do this," but when you say, "Do that" and demonstrate an action, she must remain frozen. For example, you say, "Do this!" and place your hands on your head; your child copies your actions. Then you say, "Do that!" and stand on one leg. Your child must remain frozen with her hands on her head. If she doesn't, she's out. Have your child be the leader and you follow her actions.

Beanbag Tick-Tack-Toe

This game is best for preschoolers who understand the game of tick-tack-toe. Beanbag tick-tack-toe is more challenging than regular tick-tack-toe because your aim might not let you mark the square you want!

Masking tape
10 beanbags (5 each in 2 different colors) or 2 beanbags
and 5 pennies and 5 dimes

Use tape to make a three-by-three square grid on the floor. Explain to your child that the goal is to toss three beanbags in a horizontal, vertical, or diagonal line, one beanbag per square. Stand several feet away from the grid and take a few practice throws before beginning the game. Take turns throwing beanbags onto the grid. If using only two beanbags, use a penny to mark the square where one player's beanbag lands and a dime to mark where the other player's beanbag lands. Play until one player gets tick-tack-toe or the game is deadlocked.

Group Activities

Rainy, snowy, or chilly days are great times to invite a friend or two over to play with your child. While the children may enjoy coloring, drawing, playing house, baking, or making a craft, be sure to include some active games in their play, too, such as those that follow.

Caution: Some of the following activities require balloons. Balloon pieces can pose an extreme choking hazard for young children, so any balloon play must be carefully supervised.

Partner Ball

1 large ball or balloon per pair of players

Divide the children into pairs and give each pair a ball. Have each pair face each other and hold the ball in place between their tummies. Have the partners hold hands and walk around the room without dropping the ball. How fast can they move? Can they walk in the opposite direction?

Silly School

Choose one child to be the teacher. The teacher stands before the other players (the students) and says the following rhyme:

Silly school has now begun.
No more laughing, no more fun.
If you show your teeth or tongue,
Your time is up; you are done.

The teacher then pulls faces, makes silly movements, or does anything else to try to get her students to laugh. Students who laugh must do whatever the teacher tells them to do: hop on one leg, jump up and down like a monkey, crab-walk across the room, and so on.

Upset the Fruit Basket

This game is great for a large group of children.

Chairs, mats, or sheets of paper
  (one fewer than the number of players)

Arrange the chairs facing inward in a large circle on the floor. Choose one child to be the Farmer and have her stand in the center of the circle while the other children sit on the chairs around her. Give each child one of four fruit names: apple, orange, strawberry, or banana (use only two or three fruit names for a smaller group). The Farmer then calls out a fruit; for example, "Banana!" All the bananas scramble to exchange seats with other bananas while the Farmer tries to grab an empty seat. If she fails to get a seat, she remains the Farmer for another round; if she gets a seat, she becomes a banana and the banana without a seat becomes the Farmer.

Scoop Ball

Utility knife
Gallon-size
  plastic jug
  for each
  player (a
  bleach bottle
  works best)
Duct tape
1 tennis ball for
  each player

Cut each jug into two pieces by inserting the knife just below the bottom of the handle and cutting diagonally down one side to the opposite bottom corner. Cut down the other side in the same way and recycle the bottom piece. Tape the cut edge of the other half to avoid injury.

Have the children all stand or sit in a circle. Give each child a scoop. Give one child a ball and have her toss the ball to the next player, who tosses it to the next player, and so on. Give another ball to the first child and have her start another round. Continue adding balls to the circle until there are the same number of balls in play as there are players. How fast can they pass the balls?

Circle Throw

Beanbag or ball

Have the children form a circle at least six feet in diameter (wider for older children). Choose one child to stand in the center of the circle and throw the beanbag to another child, who catches the beanbag and throws it back to the child in the center. The child in the center throws the beanbag to the next child, who catches and returns it, and so on around the circle. When all the children have caught and thrown the ball, choose a new child to stand in the center and begin again.

Sponge Toss

Several sponges (at least one per player)
Rope

Lay rope on the floor in the middle of the playing area to divide it in two. Divide the children into two teams and give each team half the sponges. Have each team stand on either side of the rope. At your signal, have the children toss the sponges to the other side—and keep tossing sponges from their sides, including those thrown by the other team, until you call stop. Count the sponges lying on each side; the team with the fewest sponges on its side wins.

Active Telephone

In the traditional game of Telephone, children sit in a circle and whisper a message from child to child. By the time the message returns to the first child, it has changed considerably. This is a physical version of the game.

Have the children stand facing outward in a circle. Choose one child to start the game. That child taps the shoulder of the child next to her, and both children turn to face the inside of the circle. The first child does a movement like hopping, jumping in place a certain number of times, or balancing on one foot with the other leg extended behind her. After demonstrating this movement, the first child faces outward. The second child then taps the shoulder of the child next to her, who turns to face the inside of the circle. The second child demonstrates the movement, then faces outward, and the third child taps the shoulder of the next player, and so on. When the last child is ready to do the movement, all the children face inward to see whether it has changed from the original movement.

Sheet Fun

Sheet or tablecloth
Several balloons in different colors (optional)

Have each child firmly grab the edge of the sheet and lift it up. Have the children walk in a circle to the right then to the left. Have them wave the sheet. If you like, inflate balloons and place them on the center of the sheet. Have the children shake the sheet to try to bounce the balloons off.

Variation: Give each child a balloon in a different color, or assign two or three children to one color. Place all the balloons on the center of the sheet. Have the children shake the sheet to try to bounce the balloons off. The color of the last balloon on the sheet denotes the winner(s).

Stack the Beanbags

Several beanbags, individually wrapped rolls of
toilet paper, wooden blocks, unopened cans of tuna,
or other stackable objects

Divide the children into two or more teams of equal size and
have teammates stand side by side in a row. At one end of each
row, place an equal number of beanbags. At your signal, the
first child in each row picks up a beanbag and passes it to the
next child, who passes it to the next child, and so on down the
row. The last child stacks the beanbags. When the last beanbag
has been stacked, the teammates sit. The first team to sit wins.

Variation: Have the children form lines rather than rows.
Teammates pass the beanbags over their heads or between
their legs to the players behind them and stack the beanbags
at the end of the lines.

Beanbag Relay

One beanbag for each team

Divide the children into two or more teams of equal size. Have each team form a line and give a beanbag to the first player in each line. At your signal, each first player lifts the beanbag either over her head or over her shoulder and drops it behind her. The second child picks it up and drops it behind her in the same way, continuing until the beanbag reaches the end of the line. The last player picks up the beanbag, runs to the front of the line, and drops it behind her, and so on down the line again. When the child who was originally first in line is now the last, she picks up the beanbag, runs to the front of the line, and the team sits. The first team to sit wins.

Olympics

To while away the hours of a long rainy day, how about organizing a series of indoor Olympic events? Consider including the following games or think up your own:

- Long jump: Have the children jump forward, with feet together, from a start line. Mark each jump with a penny or other marker. Who can jump the farthest?
- Discus throw: Have the children throw paper-plate discuses into a laundry basket. Who can hit the target?
- Have the children throw javelins (empty gift-wrapping tubes) across a line or into a target. Whose throw can cross the line or hit the target?
- Shot put: Have the children throw beanbags or balloons from a start line. Who can throw the farthest ?

Battleship

Several Ping-Pong balls, beanbags, or individually
* wrapped rolls of toilet paper*
2 laundry baskets or large cardboard boxes
Paper and pencil (optional)

Divide the children into two teams. Have each team stand
with a laundry basket at opposite ends of the room or about
eight to ten feet apart. Give one team the balls and have the
teammates try to throw as many into the other team's laundry
basket as they can. If you like, keep score by giving the team one
point for each ball that lands in the basket. Give the other
team all the balls and have the teammates try to throw as
many into the first team's basket as they can. The team with
the most points wins.

Walking Races

You don't have to run a race. You can walk a race, too! Have the children try these walking races:

- Walk on heels only.
- Walk heel to toe.
- Walk backward.
- Walk with a balloon or beanbag between the knees.
- Walk on tiptoe.
- Walk with giant steps.
- Walk while balancing a beanbag on the head.

Pass the Ball Race

1 ball per team
1 basket per team

Divide the children into two or more teams of equal size. Have the teams stand in lines, one teammate behind another with legs slightly spread. Set each team's basket behind the last players in line. Give a ball to the first player in each line. At your signal, these players pass the balls between their legs to the players behind them. The last player in each line runs to the front of the line and continues passing the ball. When the player who was originally first in line is now the last, she places the ball in her team's basket, runs back to her team, and they all sit. The first team to sit wins.

Variation: Have teammates pass the ball over their heads instead of between their legs.

Skooch Races

Masking tape or string

Make a start and finish line with the tape or string. Have each child sit on the floor at the start line, legs stretched out and arms folded across the chest. At your signal, the children must use only the muscles in their rear ends to move themselves forward to the finish line. The first child to cross the finish line wins.

Hankie Hop

Masking tape or string
1 hankie or other lightweight cloth per player

Make a start and finish line with the tape or string. Have each child lay a hankie on one foot. At your signal, players hop toward the finish line. If a player's hankie falls off her foot, she must pick it up, return to the start line, and begin again. The first player to cross the finish line with a hankie on her foot wins.

Variation: Divide a large number of children into teams and run this race as a relay.

Marshmallow Races

Masking tape or string
1 chair per team
1 large marshmallow per player

Divide the children into two or more teams of equal size. Make a start line with the tape or string. Set the chairs in a row, facing the start line, near the other end of the room. Have the teammates stand one behind another at the start line and hold their marshmallows between their knees. At your signal, the first players in line run to their chairs, around them, and back to the start line—all while keeping their marshmallows between their knees. If a player's marshmallow falls, she must begin again from the start line. When the first player has run the course, the second player begins. The first team to have all its teammates run the race wins.

Racing Fun

Races are great ways for kids to use up excess energy. Have the children race in one or more of the following ways, or have them make up their own ways to race:

- Crawl
- Hop
- Crab-walk
- Somersault

Here are some other racing ideas:

- Divide the children into pairs. Tie together the inside legs of each partner, and have the pairs compete in a three-legged race.
- Divide the children into pairs and have the pairs leapfrog to the finish line.

Chapter 4

Creative Movement

Movement is as necessary to mental
and physical development as food.

—Grace Nash

Creative movement and dance are enjoyable ways for a young child to express himself and develop his physical skills. They also provide outlets for his energy, stimulate his imagination, and promote creativity. Plus, dancing around your home is a great activity for a rainy afternoon and a wonderful way to be silly and spontaneous with your child.

Don't worry if you're not very musical or don't have a large music collection. Borrow recordings in a variety of styles from friends or from your local library. (You may want to purchase your child's favorites so they're always on hand.) Start a collection of simple props you can use with your child. Make ankle bells by stringing bells onto a length of elastic and tying the ends. Gather feathers and lightweight scarves for your child to wave and twirl. Find a soft rubber ball that your child can bounce indoors. Make or buy simple musical instruments.

The activities in this chapter will provide hours of fun and give your child opportunities to express himself through creative movement and dance.

Rhythm and Dance

Music naturally motivates young children to move; just play a lively tune and watch your child respond to the rhythm. He can hardly stop himself from bouncing and rocking to the beat!

If your child's day is already filled with lots of music and movement, great! If not, try to make music and movement activities a part of his daily life. Remember that listening and moving to music will help your child develop a sense of rhythm, improve his coordination, and practice his large and small motor skills.

Marching Fun

Recording of marching band music (Try works by John Phillip Sousa or "Seventy-six Trombones" from the musical The Music Man.*)*
Flags (optional)
Scissors and red construction paper (optional)

Play some marching band music. Join your child as he marches in place then marches around the room in time to the music. Be sure to march with your knees high. If you like, twirl or wave flags and march in a pretend parade. You and your child can pretend to beat a drum, play a trombone, crash cymbals, or conduct the band!

Variation: Cut out paper stop signs and lay them on the floor. March around the room; when you reach a stop sign, march in place for a few beats before marching on.

Stop and Go

Action Cube (optional; see Appendix)
Recordings of music (try children's music, classical,
  folk, and other styles of music)

Roll an Action Cube or choose a locomotor movement like
galloping, skipping, hopping, and so on. Play the music and
have your child move around the room in the chosen way
while the music plays. Tell him that when the music stops, he
must sit on the floor, lie on his back, balance on one foot, or
freeze in whatever position you choose. Roll the Action Cube
again or choose a new movement, put on another recording,
and play again.

Bouncing Beat

Recording of music with a strong beat
1 large ball for each person

Help your child count in time to the music. When he's able to
count the beat, show him how to bounce a ball as you count. If
you like, change the beat by counting half time or double time.

Variation: Have your child hop, jump, or skip around the
room in time to the music while holding the ball above his
head or in front of him.

Ball Toss

Recording of music with a strong beat
Ball

Listen to the music for a while and help your child hear the beat by counting it out as you listen. When he can count the beat with you, stand facing your child a few feet away from him. Toss the ball to him on the count of "one." Have him catch or retrieve the ball then toss it back to you on the next count of "one." If it'll help your child, say "toss" on the first count of the beat; for example, "*Toss*, two, three, four." For fun, try rolling or kicking the ball instead of tossing it.

Wind-Up Toys

Have your child pretend to be a wind-up toy with an imaginary key on his back. After you "wind him up," he should move quickly and animatedly, then gradually move slower and slower until he stops. Think of different kinds of wind-up toys your child could be: a marching soldier, a dancing ballerina, a galloping horse, a crawling baby doll, a monkey crashing cymbals, and so on.

Dance and Fall Down

*Recordings of music (try children's, classical, country
and western, and so on)*

Play some music and dance around the room with your child.
When a song ends, you both fall down. When the next song
begins, you both get up and dance some more. Change the
music and play again. For fun, vary the tempo (slow, medium,
and fast) and volume of the music.

Show Me a Story

Storybook (optional)

Have your child tell a familiar story (for example, "Goldilocks
and the Three Bears," "Little Red Riding Hood," or another
story) by acting it out with his body. If you like, act out the
tale with your child, using body movements as well as facial
expressions. Use words, if you like. If your child prefers, read
a storybook and have him act out the tale as you read.

Walking Fun

How many ways can your child walk? Have him try walking in the following ways:

- stiffly like a robot
- wobbly like a baby
- quickly like a speed walker
- heavily like a giant
- lightly like a ballerina on tiptoe

If necessary, describe how to move; for example, say, "Let's pretend we're robots. We're made of metal and our arms and legs are stiff and can't bend. We move very stiffly like this." Think of other ways your child might walk.

Clapping Game

Recording of music

Listen to music with your child and clap your hands to the beat in the following ways:

- Clap once in front of your waist and have your child do the same. Clap behind your back, above your head, behind your knees, and so on. Have your child copy your movements.
- Clap twice in front of your waist, above your head, behind your knees, and so on, and have your child do the same.
- Clap twice in different positions; for example, clap once above your head, then clap once in front of your waist. Have your child do the same.
- Vary how you clap. Clap loudly and softly, slowly and quickly.

Mirror Dance

Recording of music (optional)

If you like, play some music as you stand facing your child. Lift your left arm and have your child lift his right arm, copying your movement as if he were your reflection in a mirror. Do other movements with your hands and arms, and have your child copy them. If you like, do movements with your feet, legs, and head. Let your child lead and you copy his movements.

Ball Exercises

Recording of lively music
1 ball per person

Show your child how to do the following activities in time to the music:

- Hold the ball with straight arms and move it in a large circle, starting above your head, moving it down to your waist, and bringing it above your head again.
- Hold the ball above your head and sway from side to side.
- Hold the ball above your head and keep your legs straight as you bend at the waist to touch the floor with the ball.
- Hold the ball in front of you and run in place.
- Hold the ball above your head and jump in place.
- Hold the ball in front of you and hop on one foot then the other.
- Sit with stretched legs out on the floor and touch the ball to your toes, then your tummy.
- Sit with stretched legs out on the floor and hold the ball to your tummy. Bend your knees and bring your feet in close to your body, then straighten your legs and repeat.

Think of more movements to do as the music plays.

Statues

Recording of music

Play the music and show your child how to do an exercise movement like side bends, jumping jacks, or toe touches in time to the music. When you stop the music, your child must freeze. Start the music again and do a different exercise movement.

Music and Feelings

Recordings of music in various styles

This activity lets your child experience movement as it relates to music or rhythm. Play different styles of music and have your child move in a way that matches the music. For example, he can run to fast music, tiptoe to soft music, hop and bounce for happy music, and so on. Have him use his body to express the way the music makes him feel. For example, he can puff out his chest and spread his arms wide to music that makes him feel big, or he can curl into himself to music that makes him feel small.

Dance Streamers

Long lengths of brightly colored ribbon or plastic
Empty key chain or plastic shower curtain ring
Stapler
6 or more 2-foot lengths
  of crepe paper
Masking tape
Lightweight scarf
Recording
  of music

Make dance streamers in one or more of the following ways:

- Tie ribbon to an empty key chain or plastic shower curtain ring.
- Staple together lengths of crepe paper and cover the end with tape to make a handle.
- Give your child a lightweight scarf. If the scarf is too long, tie a knot in the middle to make a handle.

Let your child wave and twirl his streamers up, down, and all around as he moves in time to the music.

Move to the Music

Recording of lively music

Play the music and have your child practice hopping, skipping, galloping, leaping, and so on to the beat. Have your child vary his speed and change direction (forward, backward, sideways, circular). Have him move in straight, curved, and zigzag paths.

Nature Play

Dance streamer (see page 181) or length of ribbon

How many ways can your child move his dance streamer or ribbon to imitate nature? Have him try the following movements:
- Move the ribbon in an arc from one side of his body to the other to make a rainbow.
- Shake the ribbon in front of his body to make ocean waves.
- Hold the ribbon above his head and sway from side to side to make tree branches in a windstorm.
- Spin around and raise and lower the ribbon to make a tornado.
- Drag the ribbon across the floor to make a river.
- Run and hold the ribbon above his head to make a soaring eagle, crouching to the ground and standing back up again to catch prey.

Let's Pretend

Young children love to use their imaginations, and many spend a lot of time engaged in pretend play. Children enjoy mimicking things or tasks they see in everyday life: playing house, taking care of babies, driving toy cars, imitating the family dog, and so on. This kind of creative play lets children put themselves in the places of others while using their minds, bodies, and imaginations.

The activities in this section will encourage your child to combine movement with dramatic expression and to use his body to communicate an image, idea, or feeling.

Getting There

Have your child pretend to use different modes of transportation to get around the room. He can pretend to:

- Ride a bicycle.
- Ride a skateboard or surfboard.
- Drive a car.
- Ride a horse.
- Paddle a canoe.
- Fly an airplane.
- Parachute.
- Hang-glide.

Hopping Chant

Have your child hop to a destination as you clap to the following chant:

> Hop, hop, and do not stop
> Until you reach the (window, bookshelf, backdoor, or wherever)

If you like, change *hop* to another movement word so your child can practice skipping, crawling, galloping, and so on.

Shadow Dancing

Flashlight
Recording of music

Dim the lights in the room and shine the flashlight on a wall.
Play the music and have your child move and dance in front of
the light to cast shadows on the wall.

Animal Fun

Have your child move like a variety of creatures. For example,
say to him, "Let's pretend you're a frog. Can you hop like a frog?"
or "Let's pretend you're a giraffe. Stretch your neck really long
so you can eat leaves from the highest tree branches." Your
child will have fun slithering like a snake, crawling like a
turtle, swimming like a fish, scurrying like a crab, galloping
like a horse, flying like a bird, and so on.

Turtle Time

Large laundry basket or plastic wading pool

Have your child crawl under a large laundry basket or a plastic wading pool to make a "shell" for his back. Encourage your turtle to do the following movements:
- Crawl across the floor slowly and steadily.
- Crawl as quickly as he can to a destination while keeping his shell on.
- For more than one child, let them turtle race against each other.

Primate Walk

Have your child stand with his feet shoulders' width apart, then have him bend at the waist and rest his fists on the floor. Tell him to keep his knees and legs straight and walk around the room on his feet and fists while grunting like a gorilla.

Encourage him to hop like a monkey from one foot to another while holding his arms slightly to the side, bending them at the elbow, and quickly raising and lowering his shoulders. Don't forget the monkey sounds!

Elevator

Show your child how to pretend to be an elevator. Bend your knees and slowly squat with arms stretched out to the sides. As you lower your body, call out, "Going down!" and the number of the floors as you pass them. When you reach the bottom, hold the squat for as long as you can before calling out "Going up!" and slowly return to a standing position.

Garden Walk

Several empty soda bottles

Show your child how to create a pretend garden by "planting" empty soda bottles around the room. Go for a walk in your garden and admire your "plants and trees." If you like, try skipping, hopping, jumping, galloping, and so on around the garden.

Weather Walk

Have your child show you how he'd move about in various types of weather. For example, he could:

- Run, jump, and play in the snow.
- Cover his head and scurry through the rain, or stop to splash in a puddle.
- Lean and walk into a strong wind.
- Walk slowly in hot, sticky air while wiping his brow.
- Shiver and wrap his arms around himself as he bustles in chilly air.
- Twirl around quickly and move from side to side as if in a hurricane.
- Move slowly and blindly as if through a blizzard.

What Am I?

Think of a variety of objects in action that your child can pretend to be:
• bread popping out of a toaster
• scissors cutting paper
• a balloon filling with air then popping
• a ball rolling

Act out the objects together, or take turns acting and guessing.

Carnival of the Animals

Recording of Camille Saint-Saëns's symphony Carnival of the Animals

Play the recording of the symphony. Have your child move as the music makes him feel: royal and majestic like the lion, slow and lumbering like the elephant, stately and graceful like the swan, and so on.

If you can, get a copy of Barrie Carson Turner's *Carnival of the Animals* by Saint-Saëns, a beautiful book and CD set that you and your child will enjoy looking at and listening to together.

Cloud Hopping

Several Hula-Hoops or masking tape
Recording of soft, slow, restful music
Dance streamer (see page 181) or length of ribbon

Lay the Hula-Hoops on the floor or use masking tape to make cloud shapes on the floor. Make sure the "clouds" are far enough apart so your child can reach them by jumping, hopping, or leaping but not by stepping. Play the music, give your child a dance streamer or ribbon, and have him jump from cloud to cloud, waving his ribbon "rainbow" as he jumps.

Dodging Fun

Have your child imagine he's dodging the following objects:
- a snowball flying toward him
- a person running at him
- a door opening suddenly in front of him
- a water balloon sailing at him
- a rhino charging him

Think of other things your child can pretend to dodge. Have him try dodging when standing still and while walking, running, or skipping.

Creepy Crawly

Show your child how to pretend to be a bug. Join him as you creep and crawl around the room.

- Scurry along on your hands and knees like a busy ant.
- Lie on your tummy on the floor with your legs stretched out behind you. Drag your legs and body forward using only your arms.
- Lie on your back or tummy on the floor, arms at your sides, and use only your body to wiggle around the room.
- Lie on your back on the floor and wave your arms and legs in the air like an upside-down beetle.
- Try crawling in different directions (forward, backward, or in a circular or zigzag path) and at different speeds.

Rockets

Show your child how to pretend to be a rocket that's blasting off. Crouch to the floor and count backward from ten. After you reach the number one, yell, "Blast off!" and jump up as high as you can. If you like, be a slow rocket and jump up very slowly, or be a quiet rocket and whisper your countdown, or be a runaway rocket and race all around the room.

Tortoise and Hare

Talk to your child about how a tortoise moves slowly and heavily and how a hare moves quickly and lightly. Pretend to be tortoises as you and your child walk in place, lifting your feet slowly from the ground. After a while, call out, "Hare!" and begin to run, lifting your knees high but still running in place. Then call out, "Tortoise!" and walk in place as slowly as you can.

Variation: Walk and run around the room rather than stay in place.

Island Hopping

Several pillows, large shapes cut from construction paper,
Hula-Hoops, or circles formed from rope or string

Place the pillows or other objects on a carpeted floor. Space
the pillows so they're jumping distance for your child.
Imagine the pillows are islands and the carpet is the ocean.
Have your child jump from island to island without falling in
the water. As he jumps, remind him to bend his knees, swing
his arms, and land with both feet at the same time.

Cross the River

2 long sticks or lengths of rope or string

To form a river, place the sticks parallel to each other and
about a foot apart. Have your child practice jumping from one
riverbank to the other, reminding him to bend his knees,
swing his arms, and land with both feet at the same time.
Widen the river by moving the sticks apart a few inches, and
have your child jump again. Keep widening the river until
your child can no longer cross it.

Variation: Try other creative ways of crossing the river:
somersaulting, crawling, skipping, galloping, and so on.

Animal Stretches

Help your child develop his stability skills as he stretches and moves like the following animals:

- Show your child how to move like an elephant. Have him stretch out his arms in front of his chest and clasp his hands together, then bend at the waist and tuck his head between his arms to make an elephant's trunk. Have him swing his trunk back and forth.
- Have your child get on his hands and knees. Tell him to arch his back and tuck his head in as he stretches like a cat. Then have him drop his tummy and crane his head up so he looks like a cow.
- Have your child get on his hands and knees, then tell him to push his bottom behind him while keeping his arms straight so he stretches like a dog awaking from a nap.
- Have your child stand and balance like a flamingo. Tell him to stretch out his arms to the sides and slowly raise one foot until the sole is resting on the side of the other knee. Have him slowly bend at the waist then come back up.

Horsy Riding

Large plain sock
Newspaper, old stockings, or fiberfill
Marker
Scissors, felt, glue, and yarn (optional)
Handle of an old broom
Large rubber band
Recording of country and western music

Stuff the sock with the newspaper, old stockings, or fiberfill. Use a marker to draw features on the horse's face. (The heel is the top of the head, and the toe is the nose.) If you prefer, cut ear, eye, nostril, and mouth shapes from felt and glue them onto the sock. Glue on yarn to make the horse's mane. Insert the broom handle into the sock and wrap the rubber band around the cuff of the sock.

Present your child with his horse and play some country and western music as he gallops around the room.

Ball Monster

Blanket or sheet
Several balls

Crouch on the floor and cover yourself with the blanket or sheet. You are the hungry ball monster! Have your child roll the balls, one at a time, toward you. Snatch the balls as they come close to or under the blanket. Roll the balls back to your child and keep on playing. For sure-fire giggles and squeals, grab a hand or foot that comes too close to the ball monster. If you like, take turns being the ball monster.

Action Songs and Rhymes

Nothing brightens a dreary, dull day better than singing action songs or acting out rhymes like those that follow. Action songs help children relate movement to music, and both action songs and rhymes help children develop their sense of rhythm. Action songs and rhymes can also help young children memorize verses and poems. Most importantly, they are great fun to do for children of all ages, whether alone or in a group, indoors or out.

Ring around the Rosey

This beloved nursery rhyme is about the bubonic plague, a terrible disease that killed many Europeans in the fourteenth century. The "ring around the rosey" refers to pinkish sores that would form on a person's body. The sores would stink, and flowers would be kept in pockets to try to cover the stench. Those who died of the disease (that is, "fell down") would be burned to ashes. Despite these grisly details, the action song remains a childhood favorite. Add the second verse to complement the first in both action and mood!

Ring around the rosey, (Hold hands with
　　your child and walk in a circle.)
A pocket full of posies,
Ashes, ashes,
We all fall down! (Fall to the floor.)

Pulling up the daisies, (Sit on
　　the floor and pretend to
　　pick flowers.)
Pulling up the daisies,
Husha, husha,
We all stand up! (Stand
　　and hold hands.)

I Can

As you recite these verses, do the actions described. Have your child join you. Be sure to give each other a lot of space!

Like a bunny I can hop.
I can spin just like a top.
I can reach, reach, reach up high,
And I almost touch the sky.

In a boat I row and row,
Sometimes fast and sometimes slow.
Now a bouncing jumping jack,
I pop up and then go back.

I sway gently in the breeze
Like the little forest trees.
I make faces like a clown,
Then I softly settle down.

Punchinello

This is a fun game to play with one child or a group of children. Choose one player to be Punchinello, then recite the following lines together. Take turns being Punchinello.

> What can you do, Punchinello, funny fellow?
> What can you do, Punchinello, funny man?

(Punchinello hops, runs in place, jumps up and down, gallops around the room, or does some other movement, which the other players copy as they say the following lines.)

> We can do it, too, Punchinello, funny fellow.
> We can do it, too, Punchinello, funny man!

Shoe Song

Sing this song to the tune of "The Mulberry Bush." Pretend to put on shoes, then move as described.

> This is the way we put on our shoes,
> Put on our shoes, put on our shoes.
> This is the way we put on our shoes
> Before we skip around town.

Repeat the verse, changing the last line to include other actions, like jumping, hopping, and running.

Teddy Bear, Teddy Bear

As you say this rhyme with your child, do the actions it describes. If you like, make up additional verses and actions and/or sing the words to the tune of "Twinkle, Twinkle, Little Star."

Teddy bear, teddy bear, turn around.
Teddy bear, teddy bear, touch the ground.

Teddy bear, teddy bear, reach up high.
Teddy bear, teddy bear, touch the sky.

Teddy bear, teddy bear, bend down low.
Teddy bear, teddy bear, touch your toe.

Around the Table We Go

Card table

Set up the table in an open space so you can move around it easily. Sing this song with your child to the tune of "The Farmer in the Dell" and perform the actions described.

Around the table we go,
Around the table we go.
All day long we sing this song.
Around the table we go.

Under the table we go...

Behind the table we go...

Marching Song

Sing this song to the tune of "Twinkle, Twinkle, Little Star." March around the room with your child in single file as you sing it. As you march, pretend to play trombones, drums, cymbals, and other marching band instruments.

See the big band in the street.
Hear the marching of their feet.

They are playing as they go,
Marching, marching, to and fro.

See the big band in the street.
Hear the marching of their feet.

Skip to My Lou

This is a great song for skipping around the room. If you like, make up actions to go with each verse.

Skip, skip, skip to my Lou.
Skip, skip, skip to my Lou.
Skip, skip, skip to my Lou.
Skip to my Lou, my darlin'.

Lost my partner, what'll I do?
Lost my partner, what'll I do?
Lost my partner, what'll I do?
Skip to my Lou, my darlin'.

I'll get another one prettier than you…

Can't get a red bird. Jay bird'll do…

Fly's in the buttermilk. Shoo, fly, shoo…

Jelly in the Bowl

Sing this funny song to the tune of "The Farmer in the Dell."
Help your child think up additional verses and actions.

Jelly in the bowl,
Jelly in the bowl, (March in place.)
Wibble, wobble, wibble, wobble, (Wiggle and flail arms around.)
Jelly in the bowl. (March in place again.)

Water in the pail,
Water in the pail, (Pretend to carry a pail of water in each hand.)
Splishy, splashy, splishy, splashy, (Pretend to throw the water on each other.)
Water in the pail. (Pretend to wring the water out of your clothes
    into the pail.)

Frogs in the pond,
Frogs in the pond, (Crouch like a frog.)
Hippity, hoppity, hippity, hoppity, (Jump up and down.)
Frogs in the pond. (Crouch like a frog again.)

If You're Happy and You Know It

This well-known action song is sure to brighten any day!

If you're happy and you know it, hop around.
If you're happy and you know it, hop around.
If you're happy and you know it, then your face will surely show it.
If you're happy and you know it, hop around.

If you're happy and you know it, jump up high...

If you're happy and you know it, shake your leg...

If you're happy and you know it, skip, skip, skip...

If you're happy and you know it, clap your hands...

If you're happy and you know it, touch your toes...

Head, Shoulders, Knees and Toes

This action song is well known and well loved. Sing it and touch the body parts first very slowly, then very quickly. Or start slowly and gradually sing faster. Sing the song with your child as you walk or skip around the room, lie on the floor, stand on one foot, and so on.

> Head, shoulders, knees and toes, knees and toes.
> Head, shoulders, knees and toes, knees and toes.
> And eyes and ears and mouth and nose.
> Head, shoulders, knees and toes, knees and toes.

This Is the Way

Sing this action song with your child to the tune of "The Mulberry Bush." Do the actions described. Take turns adding verses with new actions.

This is the way I touch my head, touch my head, touch my head.
This is the way I touch my head, touch, touch, touch.

This is the way I clap my hands...

This is the way I shake my arms...

This is the way I crouch down low...

This is the way I touch my toes...

This is the way I jump up high...

This is the way I turn around...

The Wheels on the Bus

This action song is a favorite with many children. Have fun making up your own silly verses about active things that wouldn't likely be on a bus—perhaps a neighing and galloping horse or lively, chattering chimp.

The wheels on the bus go round and round, (Hold arms in front
    of you and circle each around the other.)
Round and round, round and round.
The wheels on the bus go round and round,
All around the town. (Extend arms up and out.)

The wipers on the bus go swish, swish, swish... (Sway forearms
    back and forth.)

The people on the bus go up and down... (Stand up and sit.)

The horn on the bus goes beep, beep, beep... (Press imaginary
    horn with your palm.)

The money in the bus goes clink, clink, clink... (Tilt head from side to side.)

The driver on the bus says, "Move on back"... (Move hand from in
    front of you to behind.)

The babies on the bus go, "Wah, wah, wah"... (Rub eyes with fists.)

Pop! Goes the Weasel

Chair
Action Cube (optional; see Appendix)
Large cardboard box (optional)

Place a chair in the middle of an open space so you can walk around it easily. Say the verse together with your child, and clap when you say, "Pop!" Reverse directions and repeat the verse. If you like, throw an Action Cube to determine how you'll move around the chair, or think up your own ways to move, like skipping, hopping, walking backward, and so on.

All around the cobbler's bench,
The monkey chased the weasel.
The monkey thought 'twas all in fun.
Pop! goes the weasel.

Variation: Use a large cardboard box instead of a chair and have your child crouch inside it. When you say, "Pop!" tell him to jump up.

Hokey-Pokey

This traditional action song has been a longtime favorite of many. Have fun singing it with your child and performing the actions.

> You put your right hand in, you put your right hand out;
> You put your right hand in, and you shake it all about.
> You do the Hokey-Pokey, and you turn yourself around.
> That's what it's all about!
>
> You put your left hand in...
>
> You put your right foot in...
>
> You put your left foot in...
>
> You put your right shoulder in...
>
> You put your left shoulder in...
>
> You put your right elbow in...
>
> You put your left elbow in...
>
> You put your head in...
>
> You put your whole self in...

Looby Loo

Join hands with your child and walk in a circle for the chorus of this song, then perform the action described for each verse.

Chorus

Here we go looby loo.
Here we go looby lie.
Here we go looby loo.
All on a Saturday night.

Verse

You put your right hand in;
You take your right hand out.
You give your hand a shake, shake, shake,
And turn yourself about.

Repeat the chorus, then repeat the verse for each part of the body featured in "Hokey-Pokey" on page 210.

Row, Row, Row Your Boat

Sit on the floor with your child so you're facing each other. Stretch your legs out and apart so you can hold hands. Pull your child toward you, then lean forward and have him lean back. Continue moving back and forth as you sing this familiar song. Adjust the motion to match the words of each verse.

Row, row, row your boat gently down the stream.
Merrily, merrily, merrily, merrily, life is but a dream.

Row, row, row your boat quickly down the stream...

Row, row, row your boat slowly down the stream...

Row, row, row your boat sleepily down the stream...

Row, row, row your boat happily down the stream...

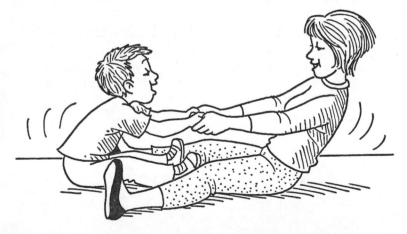

Walking through the Barnyard

Pretend to walk through a barnyard with your child. As you recite each verse, imitate the animal featured. You and your child can strut like a turkey, gallop like a horse, waddle like a duck, and so on. Make up more verses to feature other barnyard animals.

Walking through the barnyard,
What did I see?
A turkey gobbling
At me, me, me!

Walking through the barnyard,
What did I see?
A fine horse neighing
At me, me, me!

Walking through the barnyard,
What did I see?
A small duck quacking
At me, me, me!

Touching Rhyme

This action rhyme will help your child learn to name the parts of his body.

> I'll touch my hair, my lips, my eyes.
> I'll sit up straight and then I'll rise.
> I'll touch my ear, my nose, my chin,
> Then softly I'll sit down again.
>
> I'll touch my ankle, my heel, my toe.
> I'll jump up high then crouch down low.
> I'll touch my elbow, my wrist, my hand,
> I'll touch my head and then I'll stand.

Stop!

This is such a fun game to do with one toddler or a small group of toddlers. Face your child and hold his hands. Walk slowly in a circle and recite this verse as you walk.

> Round and round and round we go.
> Round and round and round we go.
> Round and round and round we go.
> Round and round and STOP!

Freeze when you say "STOP!" Repeat the game as many times as your child likes, changing directions and speeding up a little more each time.

Wiggle Song

Sing this song with your child to the tune of "The Bear Went over the Mountain" and do the actions described.

My arms are starting to wiggle,
My arms are starting to wiggle,
My arms are starting to wiggle,
As you can plainly see.

My legs are starting to wiggle...

My head is starting to wiggle...

My hips are starting
     to wiggle...

My shoulders are
     starting to wiggle...

We All Clap Our Hands Together

Sing this song to the tune of "Did You Ever See a Lassie?" (or "The More We Get Together"). Have your child do the actions described.

> We all clap our hands together, together, together.
> We all clap our hands together, as children like to do.
>
> We all turn around together...
>
> We all sit right down together...
>
> We all stand up tall together...
>
> We all stomp our feet together...

This Way and That

Sing this song with your child to the tune of "Did You Ever See a Lassie?" (or "The More We Get Together") and do the actions described.

Did you ever hop on one foot, on one foot, on one foot?
Did you ever hop on one foot, going this way and that?

Did you ever jump on two feet...

Did you ever skip in circles...

Did you ever lift your arms up...

Did you ever walk on tiptoe...

Did you ever crawl back and forth...

Did you ever stand on one foot...

Hear My Fist

As you say these verses with your child, do the actions described. Begin this rhyme while standing.

Hear my fist go thump, thump, thump
On my wide palm there.
Hear my hands go clap, clap, clap
High up in the air.

Stretch my arms out to the side
As I spin around.
Now my hands reach down, down, down
Till they touch the ground.

Quickly now I sit right down;
Pull my legs up tight.
Now I stretch them out so far,
Stretch with all my might.

See my arms go up, up, up,
Stretching up so high.
See my hands come slowly down
In my lap to lie.

My Shadow

Flashlight

Dim the other lights in the room and shine the flashlight on a wall. Say this rhyme and have your child perform the actions described in front of the light to cast shadows on the wall. Have fun making up new verses and actions.

I nod my head; he nods his head.
I skip and he skips, too.
I clap my hands; he claps his hands.
He does just what I do.

I hop three times; he hops three times.
I jump and he jumps, too.
I climb upstairs; he climbs upstairs.
We blow a kiss to you.

Nod Your Head

As you say this rhyme with your child, perform the actions described.

Nod your head, bend your knees,
Grow as tall as big oak trees.

On your knees, slowly fall,
Curl yourself into a ball.

Raise your head, jump up high,
Wave your hands, and say, "Goodbye!"

Rowing Song

Perform the actions described in each verse as you sing this song with your child. Add verses as you think of other ways to move.

Row, row, row your boat
Gently down the stream.
Merrily, merrily, merrily, merrily,
Life is but a dream.

Drive, drive, drive your car quickly down the street...

Ride, ride, ride your horse up and down the trail...

Pedal, pedal, pedal your bike all around the town...

Fly, fly, fly your plane way above the clouds...

Hopping Song

Sing this action song with your child to the tune of "Twinkle, Twinkle, Little Star." Have fun performing the actions described. If you like, sing the song again, using other action words like *jump*, *glide*, and *crawl*.

Hop and hop and hop along,
Hopping as we sing this song.
Sometimes fast and sometimes slow,
Sometimes high and sometimes low.
Hop and hop and hop along,
Hop until we've sung this song.

The Mulberry Bush

For the first verse of this song, hold hands with your child and walk in a circle. For other verses, act out the words described.

Here we go 'round the mulberry bush,
The mulberry bush, the mulberry bush.
Here we go 'round the mulberry bush
So early in the morning.

This is way we wash our clothes,
Wash our clothes, wash our clothes.
This is the way we wash our clothes
So early Monday morning.

This is the way we iron our clothes...so early Tuesday morning.

This is the way we scrub the floors...so early Wednesday morning.

This is the way we sew our clothes...so early Thursday morning.

This is the way we sweep the house...so early Friday morning.

This is the way we bake our bread...so early Saturday morning.

This is the way we go to church...so early Sunday morning.

She'll Be Coming 'Round the Mountain

New verses added to this old favorite make it a lively action song. Take turns making up verses with your child as you sing the song together.

> She'll be coming 'round the mountain when she comes.
> She'll be coming 'round the mountain when she comes.
> She'll be coming 'round the mountain,
> She'll be coming 'round the mountain,
> She'll be coming 'round the mountain when she comes.
>
> We'll all be hopping forward when she comes...
>
> We'll all be bending over when she comes...
>
> We'll be jumping up and down when she comes...
>
> We'll all be walking backward...

Group Activities

While most of the action songs and rhymes in this chapter can be played as a group activity, the following activities require several children, making them ideal for birthday parties, preschool activities, and other situations involving eight or more young children. Remind the children to show cooperation and kindness at all times when playing group games. Try to play long enough so each child gets a chance to be in the spotlight, but move to a new activity when the children begin to lose interest.

Monkey in the Middle

Choose one child to be the monkey. The other children join hands and form a circle around the monkey. While singing the following song to the tune of "The Farmer in the Dell," the children walk around the monkey. When they finish singing the song, the monkey chooses an action that everyone must do while singing the song with the new words; for example, "We all skip all around," or "We all hop on one foot," or "We all jump up and down," and so on. Play until each child has had a turn being the monkey.

The monkey's in the middle.
The monkey's in the middle.
Hi-ho the derry-o,
The monkey's in the middle.

London Bridge

Choose two children to be the bridge. Have the partners face each other, join both hands, and hold them high as the rest of the children continuously walk under the bridge in single file while singing the song. The partners gradually lower their arms until a child is caught at the phrase, "My fair lady!" The caught child then replaces one of the partners, who joins the circle.

London Bridge is falling down,
Falling down, falling down.
London Bridge is falling down,
My fair lady!

Build it up with wood and clay...

Wood and clay will wash away...

Build it up with iron bars...

Iron bars will bend and break...

Build it up with silver and gold...

Gold and silver, I have none...

Take a key and lock her up...

Set a man to watch all night...

Quick Feet

1 sheet of newspaper for each child
Recording of lively music

Spread the sheets of newspaper on the floor. Have the children run, crawl, hop, skip, and so on around the room as the music plays. When you stop the music, all the children must quickly find a sheet to stand on. Play the music again and as the children move about, remove one sheet. When the music stops, two children must share a sheet. Continue on, always removing one sheet, until all the children are standing on one sheet. If many children are playing, you may wish to quit while there are still several sheets on the ground.

Musical Hugs

Recording of lively music

Play the music and have the children dance around the room. After a while, stop the music and have each child find a partner to hug. (Group hugs are okay, too!) Start the music again, and have the children dance some more, then find another partner to hug when the music stops.

Three Blind Mice

This is a great game for a very large group of children.

3 scarves or bandanas

Choose three children to be the mice and blindfold them. Have the other children join hands and walk around the blindfolded mice while singing this classic song.

Three blind mice, three blind mice.
See how they run! See how they run!
They all ran after the farmer's wife,
Who cut off their tails with a carving knife.
Did you ever see such a sight in your life
As three blind mice?

After the song is finished, tap the heads of three children in the circle. These children each call out the name of a different mouse. The mice then try to tag the children who called their names. If the mice are successful, they change places with the children who called their names, and the game begins again.

Variation: If there is a small group of children, choose only one mouse to blindfold.

Jack Be Nimble

Small unlit candle in candleholder
Several books

Have the children line up and take turns jumping over the candle while saying the nursery rhyme:

Jack be nimble, Jack be quick
Jack jump over the candlestick!

Once all the children have jumped, place a book under the candleholder to raise it and have the children jump again. Add a book to the pile before each round. If a child knocks over the candle, remove all the books and start again with the candle-holder on the floor.

Variation: Have the child who knocks over the candle sit out. When another child knocks over the candle, he trades places with the child sitting out. If you want to declare a winner, have the children who've knocked over the candle sit out until there's only one player left in the game.

Skipping Game

Several slips of paper or index cards
Pencil
Glue (optional)
Pictures of animals (optional)

On separate slips of paper or index cards, write a different instruction, such as "Hop on one foot," "Crawl," "Run," "Dance," and so on. Scatter the slips face-down on the floor. Have the children skip around the room singing the following song to the tune of "Skip to My Lou:"

> Lost my paper, what'll I do?
> Lost my paper, what'll I do?
> Lost my paper, what'll I do?
> Skip to my Lou, my darlin'.

At the end of the verse, each child stops and picks up the slip nearest to him. Help the children read the instructions, then have them return the slips to the floor and move how instructed during the next round of play.

Variation: Glue a picture of a different animal onto each index card and have each child move like the animal pictured.

Chapter 5

Water Fun

*Whether you believe you can
do a thing or not, you are right.*

—Henry Ford

Most young children love playing in water. Whether they're
taking a bath, helping you in the kitchen, or playing in the
kiddie pool outdoors, water fascinates and delights them.
Spend even a little time with a toddler or preschooler, and
you're sure to discover this fact!

A child's natural affinity for water makes water play an
excellent way to develop large motor skills. Water adds resist-
ance when you move in it, strengthening muscles and bones.
Water play can also help develop small motor skills; handling
wet objects promotes manipulative and coordination skills.
Lastly, playing in water is just plain fun!

For your child's safety, it's important that she feels comfortable
(but not overly confident) around water. Begin introducing her
to the water at an early age and teach her basic water safety and
rules when she can understand them. If you like, enroll her in
swimming lessons or take her swimming regularly. Finally,
make sure you supervise your child around water at all times.

Caution: Some of the following activities require balloons.
Balloon pieces can pose an extreme choking hazard for very
young children, so any balloon play must be carefully supervised.

Backyard Activities

Outdoor play every day is essential for a child's physical development. With warm weather and water, the following activities make playing outdoors a treat!

Water Crawl

Small plastic bowl or container
Ice cubes (optional)

Fill the bowl or container with water. Have your child get on her hands and knees, and balance the bowl of water on her back. Choose an object in the yard, then have her crawl to it and back without spilling any water. If you like, have her crawl in a straight, curved, or zigzag path.

Variation: Substitute ice cubes for the water. Have two or more children race each other, or divide a large group of children into teams and have a relay race.

Balloon Kick

Balloon
Scarf or handkerchief

Fill a balloon with water, tie the end securely, and place it on the ground. Blindfold your child, turn her around several times, then have her try to kick the water balloon. You may let her locate the balloon with her hands before she kicks, or she can simply kick until she makes contact with the balloon. Move away from her and have her try to kick the balloon to you by following your voice.

Water Ball

Balloon
Plastic golf club or baseball bat

Fill the balloon with water, tie the end securely, and place it on the ground. Have your child swing the golf club at the balloon. If you like, pitch the water balloon to your child and have her hit it with the baseball bat. Have your child try varying the speed and force of her swings.

Sponge Balancing

Large wet sponge

Have your child use the
sponge to try one or more
of the following activities:

- Balance it on her head
  while walking.
- Balance it on her head
  while standing on one foot.
- Balance it on her head
  while climbing stairs.
- Stand on one foot and balance the sponge on her knee.
- Balance it on her outstretched hand and walk or run
  forward and backward.
- Balance it on her back and crawl across the lawn.

Racquet Fun

Small wet sponges or small filled water balloons
Child's tennis racquet

Have your child practice hitting the sponges or water balloons
with a tennis racquet. You may wish to pitch the object to her
or she may prefer to try hitting it on her own. Show her how
to drop the object from one hand and hit it underhand. (Most
young children can't throw the object in the air and hit overhand.)

Water Target Practice

Sponges
Chalk
Spray paint and sheet
of plywood (optional)
Several old buckets or
large plastic containers
Permanent marker

Wet the sponges then use them in one of the following ways:

• Use chalk to draw a target on a fence or pavement. Have your child throw a sponge and try to hit the target. Then ask her to aim for a spot in front of or beyond the target. (The sponge will wash the chalk away quickly; if your child enjoys this activity, consider spray-painting a target on a sheet of plywood that you can lay flat or prop against a wall or fence.)

• Place a bucket some distance away from your child. Have her try to throw the wet sponges into the bucket. Ask her to throw slower and faster.

• Line up several buckets or plastic containers. Use a permanent marker to label each bucket with a symbol your child will recognize (a letter, number, or picture). Have your child try to throw the sponges into specific buckets.

Bottle Fun

Large bucket or container
Funnels and cups
Empty 2-liter soda bottle with cap
Wagon

Fill the bucket with water. Show your child how to place a funnel into the soda bottle, scoop water from the bucket with a cup, and pour it through the funnel to fill the bottle. When the bottle is full, your child may like to do one of the following activities:

- Dump the water back into the bucket.
- Cap the bottle and carry it around the yard to "water" the flowers, trees, or other objects. Or place it in a wagon, and pull it around the yard.
- Cap the bottle and roll it in the grass or along the driveway.

Ice Cube Play

Food coloring
Several water balloons or small milk cartons
Bucket or plastic container
Hula-Hoop
Plastic golf club

Make colored ice cubes by adding food coloring to the water before you freeze it. To make giant ice cubes, fill and freeze several water balloons or small milk cartons. Use the ice cubes in one or more of the following ways:

- Set a bucket several feet away from your child. Have her try to throw the ice cubes into it. Have her vary her aim; for example, ask her to throw the ice cubes so they land in front of or beyond the bucket, and have her try to throw underhand and overhand.
- Lay a Hula-Hoop some distance away from your child. Have her throw ice cubes into the hoop. If an ice cube lands outside the circle, ask her to throw another ice cube so it lands near the first.
- Have your child hit a frozen water balloon with a plastic golf club. Have her hit it with a soft, medium, then strong swing.
- Play catch with a frozen water balloon. Try tossing it high above your heads, at chest level, and down by your knees.
- Kick a frozen water balloon back and forth or toward a target. Take a few steps before kicking.

Sprinkler Aerobics

On a hot summer day, have an
aerobics class in your sprinkler.

Oscillating sprinkler
Recording of lively music
(optional)

Set up your sprinkler in an
open area. Take turns being an aerobics instructor as you run,
hop, skip, jump, gallop, bend, twist, stretch, and sway in the
water. Vary the speed and direction of your movements. If you
like, play some lively music during your class.

Water Swings

Oscillating sprinkler
Plastic kiddie pool

Set up the sprinkler close to your swing set so your child can
swing into the spray. If you like, place a plastic kiddie pool at
the bottom of the slide and fill it with water. Your child will
have fun sliding into the water.

Body Shop

Your child's toy car has been in an accident and must be repaired! Help her set up a body shop in the driveway.

Toy car or other riding toys
Toy tools
Biodegradable tempera paint
Paintbrush
Sponge and bucket or garden hose

Let your child fix her "damaged" riding toy with a toy hammer, screwdriver, and other toy tools. Once the body work is done, let her paint the riding toy. When the activity is over, use a wet sponge or garden hose to wash the paint away.

Water Catch

Wet sponge or filled water balloon

Toss a wet sponge or a water balloon back and forth with your child. Count as you throw and see what number you can get to before one of you drops the sponge or balloon.

Wash the Ride

Bucket full of warm soapy water
Rags
Sponges
Garden hose

Set a bucket of warm soapy water in your driveway. Have your child wash her riding toys with rags and sponges. Let her rinse them with the garden hose. If you like, wash your own car at the same time and have her help you.

Bike Riding

On a hot summer day, you may feel like sitting still. Adding a sprinkler will increase the incentive to get moving.

Oscillating sprinkler
Bike, trike, scooter, or in-line skates

Set up the sprinkler so it sprays over a driveway or sidewalk. Join your child as she rides her bike, trike, or scooter through the spray, or strap on some in-line skates and glide through it. Practice riding or skating slowly and quickly, and in straight, curved, and zigzag paths.

Water Balloon Basketball

Several 6- to 8-inch helium-quality balloons
Child's basketball net, laundry baskets, or other large containers

Fill the balloons with water and tie them securely. Have your child stand several feet away from a basketball net and try to throw the balloons through the net. If possible, raise and lower the net as you play and change the place from which your child throws. If using laundry baskets or other large containers, vary the heights of the containers by placing one on a picnic table, another on a chair, and another on the ground. Have your child try to throw overhand, underhand, and sideways.

Bucket Toss

Rope or chalk
5 buckets
Small ball or water balloon

Use rope or chalk to mark a start line and fill the buckets with
water. A few feet from the start line, set the buckets in a line,
one behind another, spacing them out by a few inches. Have
your child stand at the start line and try to toss a small ball into
the first bucket. If successful, have her retrieve it, return to
the start line, and try to toss the ball into the second bucket.
Have her continue tossing the ball into the buckets in order.
If the ball lands in a bucket out of order or if the ball misses
a bucket, she must start over again with the first bucket.

River Jump

Garden hose

Turn on the water to your garden hose and lay it on the ground. Tell your child the stream of water is a raging river and she must try to jump over it. Once she has jumped, raise the hose an inch from the ground and hold it so the water sprays horizontally. Have her jump again. Continue raising the stream until she can no longer jump over it without getting wet.

Variation: Start by holding the stream of water at the same height as your child's head and have her move under it however she can without getting wet. Continue lowering the stream an inch until your child gets wet.

Sprinkler Tag

Rotating sprinkler

- Stand with your child within range of a rotating sprinkler. Try to jump over the water when it reaches you. How many jumps can you make before getting wet?
- Run in a circle, trying to stay ahead of the water. How long before the water catches you?

Water Bounce

Kiddie pool
Large rubber ball

Fill a kiddie pool with several inches of water, then try the following activities:
- Have your child stand in the pool and practice bouncing the ball in the water.
- You and your child stand on opposite sides of the pool, either outside or inside the pool. Throw a ball toward your child so it bounces in the water. Have your child try to catch the ball on the rebound.
- Have your child stand outside the pool and throw the ball as hard as she can at the water. How high can she make the water splash?

Fill and Dump

Garden hose
Bucket
Wagon
Toy shovel

Toddlers love
to fill things up,
dump them out, and move heavy objects. The following ideas
will give them lots of opportunities to do all three!

- Let your toddler use a garden hose to fill up the bucket with
  water. If she can lift it, let her set the bucket in a wagon and
  pull it around the yard. Or she may just want to dump the
  bucket out and fill it up again. (If you don't like to waste
  water, have your child dump the water into a kiddie pool
  and use it to water the garden or lawn.)

- If your toddler loves to dig, have her use a toy shovel to fill
  the bucket with sand or dirt. Let her set it on a wagon to
  pull around, carry it to another part of the yard, or simply
  dump it out and start again.

Indoor Water Play

While you can modify some of the previous activities and
games for indoor play, most of them encourage the development of large motor skills and are suitable for outdoor play.
The following indoor activities, however, can encourage the
development of small motor skills and can be a wonderful way
to spend a rainy morning or a scorching summer day.

Bath Time Fun

Help your child get the most fun out of every bath by varying the items she plays with each time.

Plastic cups
Plastic kitchen utensils
Sponges (plain or cut into shapes)
Small containers
Ping-Pong ball

Put a few inches of warm water in the tub, place your child in the water, then let the tap run slowly so she can fill up cups, play in the stream of water, and so on.

- Add plastic kitchen utensils and let your child play with them in the water.
- Sponges are fun to play with in the bath.
- A toddler will love filling up small containers with water and pouring them out.
- A Ping-Pong ball can provide lots of fun in the tub. Try to keep it under the water—it will always pop up!
- Poke a few holes in the bottom of a plastic container. Your child will enjoy filling it with water and watching the water drip out the bottom.

Kitchen Water Play

The kitchen is a great place for young children to play with water, provided you're in no hurry and prepared to mop up a lot of water!

Several thick towels
Child's step stool
Plastic bowls, cups, and other containers
Bucket
Measuring cups and spoons, plastic bottles, and sponges
Dish detergent, eggbeater, and squeeze bottles (optional)

- Fill your kitchen sink with warm water, place a towel on the floor by the sink, pull up a child's step stool, and let your preschooler play in the water with plastic bowls, cups, and other containers.
- Open your clean, empty dishwasher, place several towels on the floor under the dishwasher door, set a bucket of water on the door, and let your toddler play with small cups and containers in the water.
- Place towels under a child-size table and give your child measuring cups and spoons, plastic bottles and containers, and sponges to play with in a bucket of water. If you like, add a little dish detergent, an eggbeater, and squeeze bottles.

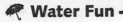
Washing the Floor

You may end up with more water on the floor than you'd like, so don't try this activity if you're short on time or have special flooring that can't be saturated.

Bucket
Sponge

Fill the bucket with an inch or two of water. Show your child how to dip the sponge into the bucket, squeeze out the excess water, then wipe the sponge across the floor to wash it. Have her try to make different shapes with the water as she moves the sponge, like a big heart, wide rainbow, or large tree. Let her crawl across the floor, squeezing and wiping, until she tires of the activity.

Ice Play

Thick towel
Baby bathtub
Large ice cubes
Colander
Plastic containers
Fishing net
Food coloring, balloons, small milk cartons (optional)

Place the baby bathtub on a towel on the floor. Fill the tub with several inches of cool water, then add the ice cubes. Have your child explore different ways of getting the ice out of the water: colanders, plastic containers, fishing net, cupped hands, toes, and so on.

Variation: Make colored ice cubes by adding food coloring to the water in the ice cube tray before you freeze it. Make really large ice cubes by freezing the water in balloons or small milk cartons.

Bathtub Simon Says

Fill the bathtub with just enough warm water so it won't cover your child's face when she lies in the tub. Have your child climb into the tub, then play a game of Simon Says with her. Say, "Simon says, 'Lay down,'" "Simon says, 'Kneel,'" "Simon says, 'Reach way up high,'" "Simon says, 'Touch your toes,'" and so on. Your child should keep still when you don't first say, "Simon says." Take turns being Simon. To avoid the risk of injury, don't include instructions that would have very young children standing in the tub, and only include such instructions for older children when there's a nonslip mat in place.

Pool Activities

While all of the following activities are suitable to do in a
swimming pool, some are also appropriate for lakes, rivers,
oceans, and other natural bodies of water. Remember that
young children should never be more than an arm's length
away from an adult when playing in water. When using public
swimming pools, check their rules before bringing in balls or
other playthings.

Dolphins

Hula-Hoop

- Hold a Hula-Hoop in the water for your child to swim or dive through. Then have her hold the hoop and you dive or swim through it.
- If your child is comfortable swimming underwater, stand with your feet wide apart in water that's as high as her chest. Have her swim between your legs.

Water Work

Try the following movements with your child in water no higher than her chest:
- Walk forward and backward.
- Walk heel-to-toe.
- Run, skip, and gallop.
- Hop from one side of the pool to the other.
- Move to shallow water and crawl through it.

Race to see who can first get from one side of the pool to the other in one of the above ways.

Water Stability

Practice some basic stability movements in the water. Try the following in water no higher than your child's chest:
- Stand on one foot.
- Hop on one foot.
- Jump with both feet.
- Run in place.
- Turn in circles in place.
- Stretch from side to side.
- Walk on tiptoe.
- Twist from side to side.

Water Ring around the Rosey

In shallow water, hold hands with your child and slowly hop in a circle as you sing the following lines:

Ring around the rosey,
A pocket full of posies.
One, two, three, four!
Get your chin wet!

Sing the verse again, but have your child put one ear in the water. Then sing it again and have her put the other ear in the water. Choose other body parts that she can put in the water. If your child is comfortable being underwater, sing the traditional nursery rhyme and fall into the water.

Water Simon Says

Play a game of Simon Says in the water with your child. Say, "Simon says, 'Float on your back,'" "Simon says, 'Blow bubbles in the water,'" "Simon says, 'Hop on one leg,'" "Simon says, 'Run in place,'" and so on. Your child should keep still when you don't first say, "Simon says." Take turns being Simon.

Water Ball Play

Beach ball or rubber ball
Ping-Pong ball

Stand in water that's as high as your child's chest and try the following activities:

- Toss a beach ball or rubber ball back and forth to each other. Try tossing it overhead with two hands, striking it with your fist, or other ways. Vary how far you stand apart and the speed with which you throw the ball.
- Try different ways of moving a Ping-Pong ball: throwing, making waves to move the ball, blowing on it, and so on.

- In shallow water, kick the beach ball across the water to each other.
- Have your child stand at the edge of the pool and kick or throw the beach ball to you in the water.

Treasure Hunt

Having a treasure hunt is a great way for a young child to become comfortable in the water.

Pennies, spray-painted rocks, strings of beads,
 bracelets, and so on
Stopwatch (optional)

For very young children or those uncomfortable in water, place the treasures in shallow water. For children who are comfortable ducking their heads underwater, place some of the treasures in deeper water. Supervise your child carefully as she searches for the treasures. If you like, time how long it takes her to find the treasures. Then drop the treasures back in the water and have her try to better her time.

Water London Bridge

In the shallow end of the pool, stand an arm's length from the side, grab the edge with both hands, and arch your arms to form a bridge. Sing "London Bridge" (see page 226) as your child passes under the bridge. Have your child vary the way in which she moves under the bridge: jump, skip, hop, run, and so on. If your child is comfortable, lower the bridge until she must put her face in the water to pass under the bridge.

Pool Races

Stopwatch
5 pennies
Balloon

Have a variety of races or competitions in the pool with your child.
- In water as high as your child's chest, how fast can she run from one side of the pool to the other?
- How fast can she pick up five pennies from the pool floor?
- How fast can she push a balloon on the surface of the water from one side of the pool to the other?
- How fast can she dog paddle from one side of the pool to the other?
- In shallow water, how fast can she crawl from one side of the pool to the other?

Group Activities

Group activities that involve water are usually big hits with young children. Activities in the water can be especially fun, but be sure to supervise the children very carefully. For groups of very young children, I recommend that there's at least one adult present for every two children. Even a shallow backyard pool can pose a risk, so make sure the children understand some basic rules: For example, children must always be within an arm's reach of an adult; they must never hold another child's head underwater; they must never compete to see who can stay under the water the longest, and so on.

Sponge Races

Wet sponges

- Have two or more children race to a finish line with the sponges on their heads or outstretched hands.
- Have two or more children stand on one foot and balance the sponges on their knees. Who can keep the sponge on her knee the longest?
- Have two or more children crawl across the yard, racing to see who can keep the sponge on her head, shoulders, or back the longest.

Water Balloon Relay

Water balloons (several per team)
Large container
Small prizes (optional)

Place the water balloons in the container. Divide the children equally into two or more teams. Have each team form a line, one teammate standing behind another. Give a water balloon to the first player in each line. At your signal, the first players pass the balloons over their heads to the next players in line, who pass them overhead to the next players, and so on until the balloons reach the last players. The last players run to the front of their lines and start a new round of passing the balloons. If a teammate drops a water balloon and it breaks, the first player in line must run to the container, get a new balloon, run back to her team and begin passing down the line again. Play continues until the player who was originally first in line is now the last. When that player receives the water balloon, she races to put it in the container, then runs to the front of her line, and the team sits down. If you like, award a prize to the first team to sit down.

Catch Contest

One water balloon for each pair of children

Have the children pair up, and have the partners face each other and stand several feet apart. At your signal, have the partners start tossing the water balloons to each other. The last pair whose water balloon doesn't break is the winner.

Water Tag

Water gun

Choose one player to be It. Define a safe zone to which players can run to avoid being tagged. It tries to tag the other players by hitting them with a stream of water. When a player is tagged, she becomes It for the next round.

Variation: Provide one water gun for each player. When a player is tagged with water, she picks up a water gun and joins It in chasing and squirting untagged players. The last player to be tagged becomes It for the next round.

Water Jump

Rotating sprinkler

Have the children stand in a circle around a rotating sprinkler. Tell them they must jump over the stream of water as it reaches them. The children can compete to see who'll be the last to get wet.

Shark

This game is a version of tag and is best played with a large group of preschoolers in a wading pool. Choose one player to be the shark. Other players try to keep away from the shark, but if the shark tags them they must either stand in place or sit at the edge of the pool. When all players have been tagged, choose a new shark and play again.

Variation: Players who have been tagged by the shark turn into seaweed; they stand in place and can tag any untagged players they can reach without moving from their spots.

Stingrays

This game is another version of tag that's best played with a large group of preschoolers in a wading pool. Choose two players to be stingrays. The other players try to keep away from the stingrays, but if a stingray tags them they must stand in place with their arms stretched out. A tagged player can be freed to play again if an untagged player ducks under her arms.

Variation: For older children or more proficient swimmers, have the children play in chest-high water. Tagged players can be freed to play again by untagged players swimming between their legs.

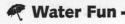

Water Limbo

Garden hose

Hold the hose so the water sprays horizontally. Begin with the stream of water at the level of the children's chins, and have each child walk under the stream. Lower the stream a bit and have the children walk under it again. Continue lowering the stream so players have to crouch, crawl, and perhaps even slither to avoid getting wet. Players are out once they get wet. The last dry player is the winner.

Bucket Brigade

4 small buckets
2 baby bathtubs
2 garden hoses

Divide the children equally into two teams. Each team should have at least four players. Give each team a baby bathtub, two buckets, and a garden hose. Arrange the teams so one player from each team stands next to a bathtub while their teammates form a line from their respective tubs to the garden hoses. Give two buckets to each of the players nearest the hoses. At your signal, the two players nearest the hoses begin to fill one of their buckets with water. When the buckets are full, the players pass them to their teammates and begin filling their second buckets. The teammates keep passing the buckets down the line until they can be dumped into the tubs, then the buckets are passed back to the garden hoses, where they are filled again. The first team to make its bathtub overflow wins.

Chapter 6
Holiday Activities

There are only two lasting bequests
we can hope to give our children.
One of these is roots, the other, wings.

—Hodding Carter

Holiday celebrations provide us with opportunities to gather with friends and family, give and receive gifts, eat traditional meals, play games, and help make happy memories for our children. And while these celebrations break up the day-to-day routine, they can also make life hectic for families with toddlers and preschoolers. Eating too many rich foods and staying up too late will often lead to irritable, tired families.

To help keep your family on an even keel, remember to set aside time for physical activity when making your holiday plans. Even a quick physical activity will help relieve tension and provide a welcome break from the hustle and bustle of your holiday preparations. For example, after baking sugar cookies for Valentine's Day, get outside for a brisk walk or snowball fight. Follow an Easter craft session with a lively game of Simon Says. Put on seasonal music and make up silly Christmas dances with your child.

This chapter provides ideas for incorporating physical activities into your holiday celebrations. While some are suitable for one child, others are great to do with family and friends. You can also modify many activities in the other chapters of this book to match your festivities simply by using holiday colors, symbols, or music.

Valentine's Day

Valentine's Day provides a wonderful opportunity to express our love to those who mean the most to us. Your child will enjoy making heart-shaped crafts and cookies, dressing in red, giving and receiving valentines, and doing the following activities. If you like, invite a few friends over for a simple Valentine's Day party. Serve heart-shaped snacks and red juice, exchange valentines, and play a few of the following games together.

Heart Balance

Scissors
Pink or red construction paper
  or plain newsprint
Marker
Recording of music (optional)

Cut out heart shapes from the construction paper or newsprint. On each heart, write a way you wish your child to balance: arms stretched out to the sides and balanced on one foot, arms stretched out to the sides and one leg extended back, one knee lifted and arms folded across the chest, and so on. Have your child jump from heart to heart and try to balance in the way that's written on each. Or play music and have him move from heart to heart. When the music stops, he must stop on a heart. Have him balance in the way that's written on the heart.

Heart Race

This heart-racing game requires two or more players.

Scissors
Pink or red construction paper or newsprint
Masking tape or string
Valentine candy or other small prize (optional)

Cut out large heart shapes from the construction paper or newsprint, two for each player. Mark a start and finish line with tape or string. Have the players stand on one of their paper hearts at the start line and hold their other hearts in their hands. At your signal, players place the hearts in their hands on the floor in front of them. Then they step onto those hearts, turn around and pick up the first hearts, place them on the floor in front of them, and step onto them. Play continues in this way until players cross the finish line. If you like, reward the first player to cross the finish line with candy or other small prize.

Valentine's Day Hop

Scissors
Recording of music (optional)
Pink or red construction paper or plain newsprint
Action Cube (optional; see Appendix)

Cut out large heart shapes from the construction paper or newsprint and scatter them on the floor. Your child will enjoy jumping from heart to heart without letting his feet touch the floor. Vary the activity by having him hop on one foot or jump backward, or have him roll an Action Cube to determine how he'll move from heart to heart.

For a group of children, play music as the children hop. Stop the music and have the children freeze until the music starts again.

Cinnamon Heart Toss

This game requires two or more players. Since children will likely eat some of the candy as you play, have them wash their hands before you begin.

Cinnamon heart candy
Small containers (1 per child)
Sheet or tablecloth
Large container
Masking tape, string, or chalk
Valentine candy or other small prize (optional)

Divide the cinnamon hearts equally among the small containers. Lay a sheet or tablecloth on the floor or ground. Set a large container in the middle of the cloth and mark a line on the floor with masking tape, string, or chalk about five feet from the large container.

Give each player a container of cinnamon hearts. Have the players take turns standing behind the line and tossing their candy at the large container. (If you like, allow younger children to stand closer and have older players stand farther away.) Allow the players four or five tosses per turn. Award a point for each heart that lands in the container.

The player who gets the most points is the winner. If you like, give the winner some Valentine candy or a small prize.

Heart Search

Individually wrapped heart-shaped candy or small paper hearts

Hide the candies or paper hearts around the room. With your child, sing the following song to the tune of "The Farmer in the Dell" as he looks for the hidden hearts. Sing the other verses, too, and do the actions described.

> I walk to find the heart.
> I walk to find the heart.
> Looking high and looking low,
> I walk to find the heart.
>
> I run to find the heart...
>
> I skip to find the heart...
>
> I jump to find the heart...
>
> I crawl to find the heart...

Catch the Heart

Scissors
Pink or red construction paper
Glue or stapler
Basket or ice-cream bucket

Prepare for the game by making hearts from pink or red construction paper: Cut strips about two inches wide and eight inches long from the construction paper. Fold the strips in half. To form a heart from each strip, open the strip slightly so the fold becomes the bottom of a V shape. Then curl the ends in to each other so they meet above the fold and glue or staple them together.

Give your child a basket or ice-cream bucket in which to catch the hearts. Throw the hearts into the air, one at a time, and have your child try to catch them. Take turns throwing and catching hearts.

Saint Patrick's Day (March 17)

Saint Patrick's Day celebrates the patron saint of Ireland. Bishop Patrick introduced Christianity to Ireland during the fifth century, and in Ireland he's still honored with a national holiday and a week of religious festivities.

Irish or not, young children will enjoy celebrating Saint Patrick's Day by having a simple celebration with family or friends. Dress in green, eat green food, make a simple craft, listen and dance to Irish music, and play a few of the following active games together.

Potato Race

One or more children can play this game.

Ropes or masking tape
1 potato per player
Small prize (optional)
Stopwatch (optional)

Mark a start and finish line with ropes or masking tape. Have the players get on their hands and knees at the start line. Place a potato in front of each player. At your signal, the players must push their potatoes across the finish line using only their noses. If you like, give a small prize to the first player to cross the finish line.

A child playing alone may try to push the potato across the finish line within a given amount of time, or he may try to better his previous times.

Variation: Have players walk with potatoes balanced on their heads or carried on spoons. Or have them crawl with potatoes balanced on their backs.

Pass the Potato

This game requires six or more players and is most suitable for older preschoolers.

1 potato per team
Large container
Small prizes (optional)

Divide the children equally into two or more teams. Have each team stand in a line with teammates one behind another. Give a potato to the first player in each line. At your signal, have teams pass their potatoes over their heads down the line. When the last players in line get the potatoes, they run to the front of their lines and continue passing. Play continues until the player who was originally first in line is now the last. When that player gets the potato, he runs to drop it into a large container. Then he runs back to his team, and they all sit down. If you like, award small prizes to the first team to sit down.

Paddy's Day Pitch

A family or group of children can play this fun game. You can decorate the game board with shamrocks, leprechauns, and other Irish symbols. Or leave it plain so you can play the game at any time.

Marker
Poster board or sheet
  of paper at least 2
  feet square
Candy, pencil erasers,
  stickers, or other
  small trinkets or toys
10 pennies per player
1 small container per player
1 small bag per player
Green construction paper, scissors, and large box (optional)

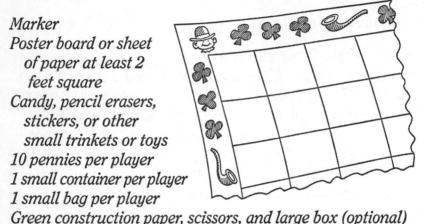

Draw a grid of three- or four-inch squares on poster board or paper. On some of the each squares, place a prize. Give each player ten pennies in a small container. The players take turns standing a distance away from the board and pitching pennies at the grid. If a player lands a penny on a square with a prize, he claims the prize in that square and collects it in his small bag.

Or cut out shamrock shapes from green construction paper, write a physical activity on each one (hop in place for 10 seconds, do 5 jumping jacks, and so on), and place the shamrocks on the squares. Keep the prizes in a box. Let players whose pennies land on the shamrock squares choose their own prizes from the box after doing the activities written on the shamrocks.

Patrick Says

While playing this game, talk with an Irish accent. Your child should follow your instructions only when you say, "Patrick says." For example, "Patrick says, 'Touch your toes'," "Patrick says, 'Stretch your arms'," "Patrick says, 'Jump up and down'." Your child should keep still when you don't first say, "Patrick says." Take turns being Patrick. Include basic locomotor movements (galloping, hopping, jumping, running, skipping, sliding) and nonlocomotor movements (bending, pulling, pushing, stretching, swaying, swinging, turning, twisting).

Green Balloon Fun

Green balloons
Tape and string
Toy bat, golf club, or rolled-up newspaper

Blow up the balloons and tie them shut, then try the following activities with your child:

- Volley a balloon to your child and have him volley it with his fingertips back to you.
- Try hitting with a closed fist underhand and overhand. How long can you keep the balloon off the ground?
- Use various body parts (foot, knee, elbow, shoulder, head, hand) to keep the balloon afloat as long as possible.
- If possible, hang balloons from the ceiling and practice hitting them with your fist or with a toy bat, golf club, or rolled-up newspaper.
- Place a balloon between your knees and race across the room.
- Kick a balloon to each other.

Caution: Balloon pieces can pose an extreme choking hazard for young children, so any balloon play with toddlers must be carefully supervised.

Easter (date varies)

Easter is a Christian holiday that celebrates the resurrection of Jesus Christ. For many, it's also a celebration of the coming spring and all its delightful signs of new life.

Easter celebrations may include a formal family dinner or an impromptu picnic in the park. Children will enjoy decorating eggs and having a candy hunt, indoors or out. Perhaps it's a good time to get the bicycles out of storage and go for a ride together. However you choose to celebrate Easter, the following games and activities will engage one or more children in some fun physical activity.

Easter Bunny Trail

Rope, two-by-four, masking tape, table, chairs,
and other obstacles
Several real, plastic, or candy Easter eggs
2 baskets or containers

Create a trail for your child to follow. Lay rope for him to walk on or jump over. Set out a two-by-four for him to balance on. Make a pathway of masking tape for him to follow. Set up a table and chairs for him to crawl under and climb over. Place the Easter eggs in a basket at the beginning of the trail. Place an empty basket at the end of the trail.

Have your child take an egg from the basket, follow the trail, and place the egg in the empty basket. Have him follow the trail back to the start, take another egg, and continue until he's delivered all the Easter eggs.

To play with more than one child, give one egg to each player and have the players take turns moving their eggs to the end of the trail.

Egg Sort

Several real, plastic, or candy Easter eggs in different colors
Easter basket
Containers in colors that match eggs

Place the eggs in the Easter basket and set it on the floor or ground. Set out the colored containers at different distances from the Easter basket. Have your child hop like a bunny as he picks an egg from the Easter basket and deposits it into the appropriately colored container. Continue until he's distributed all the eggs.

Egg Pass

This game requires six or more players.

2 containers for each team
Several real, plastic, or candy Easter eggs

Divide the children equally into two or more teams. Have each team stand in a line, with teammates either next to or behind one another. At the front of each line, set a container on the floor or ground and fill it with eggs. At the end of each line, place an empty container. At your signal, the first player on each team takes an egg from the container and passes it to the next player in line however he wishes (hand to hand, overhead, between the legs, and so on). That player passes the egg to the next player in line in a different way than it was passed to him, and so on. When the last player in the line receives the egg, he places it into the empty container. Play continues until the teams have moved all the eggs from one container to the other.

Variation: To add more physical activity to this game, have the players hop to a finish line when they've moved all their eggs.

Egg Roll

Several real, plastic, or candy Easter eggs
Baskets or other containers (optional)

Have your child practice his manipulative skills by rolling eggs in one or more of the following ways:

- Sit on the floor opposite your child, legs stretched out wide, and roll an egg back and forth to each other.
- Roll an egg toward a target.
- Have your child roll an egg across the floor with his nose, elbow, or another part of his body.
- For a group of children, have an egg-rolling race. Divide players into pairs and have each pair sit on the floor several feet apart, facing each other. Give one player in each pair a basket of eggs and the other player an empty basket. Have the pairs roll all the eggs from the full basket into the empty one. The first pair to move all the eggs wins.

Bunny Hop

Have fun hopping around the room with your child!

Recording of "The Bunny Hop" (optional)

Dance and hop with your child as you sing "The Bunny Hop" or play a recording of it. If you like, teach him the following moves: Stand with your hands on the waist of the person in front of you. As the music begins, kick twice to the right, twice to the left, jump forward, backward, forward three times, and repeat.

Spring Things

Recording of Vivaldi's "Spring" Concerto (optional)

Talk with your child about things associated with spring: baby rabbits, ducklings, eggs, flowers, rain, wind, and so on. Then have your child physically express those things. For example, he can hop like a bunny, waddle like a duck, curl up into a ball and roll around the floor like an egg, stand and stretch high like a flower growing. If you like, listen to Vivaldi's "Spring" Concerto and have your child move to the music.

Canada Day (July 1)

Canada Day is Canada's birthday. It honors the anniversary of Canada's confederation in 1867. Canada Day festivities are much like Independence Day celebrations in the United States. Family, friends, and neighbors gather for parades, picnics, barbecues, games, and fireworks at night.

Enjoy the following games and activities as you celebrate Canada Day and the arrival of summer with your child.

What Day Is It, Mr. Wolf?

This game is suitable for four or more players.

Rope

Choose one player to be Mr. Wolf. Make a start line with the rope, and have the other players stand behind it. Have Mr. Wolf stand some distance away from the players on the other side of the rope. Have him face away from the players. To begin the game, players call out, "What day is it, Mr. Wolf?" Mr. Wolf answers with the names of different holidays (Valentine's Day, Easter, Christmas, and so on). With each answer, the players take a step forward. When Mr. Wolf says, "It's Canada Day!" he turns and tries to tag the players, who try to run to safety behind the start line. If a player is tagged, he either becomes Mr. Wolf or chases the other players with Mr. Wolf until all have been caught.

Slip and Slide Bowling

Here's a fun twist on the classic summertime activity!

Large sheet of plastic or several garbage bags
  (cut open to lie flat)
Liquid dishwashing detergent
Hose or sprinkler
Empty plastic soda bottles or plastic bowling pins

Spread out the plastic sheet or garbage bags on a flat, debris-free part of your lawn. Pour a little liquid dishwashing detergent on the plastic and spray water from the hose or sprinkler on it. Set up soda bottles or plastic bowling pins at the end of the plastic. (If the soda bottles fall down too easily, fill them with a little water before setting them up.) Have your child get a running start, slide on the plastic, and try to knock over as many bowling pins as he can! Have him try sliding on his tummy, bottom, back, side, and so on. Which way knocks over the most pins?

Canadian Music and Movement

From Maritime/Celtic, to Acadian, to country and western, the music that represents Canada's heritage is rich and diverse. If you don't own any recordings of Canadian music, borrow some from friends or the library that reflect Canada's musical past and present. Listen to the music with your child and dance or move as the music inspires you.

Michael Mitchell has recorded two CDs of Canadian folk music just for kids: *Canada Is for Kids, Volumes 1 and 2*. They may be available in your local library, or you can order them online at www.michael-mitchell.ca.

Patriotic Balloon Play

Several red and white balloons
Rope (optional)

Blow up the balloons and tie them off. Volley one balloon back and forth with your child. Try hitting it with your fingertips, then hitting it with a closed fist underhand and overhand. How long can you keep the balloon off the ground? Try keeping several balloons off the ground.

Try using other body parts to keep one or more balloons afloat as long as possible, or lay a rope on the ground and volley the balloons back and forth over the rope.

Caution: Balloon pieces can pose an extreme choking hazard for very young children, so any balloon play must be carefully supervised.

Message in a Bottle

Pen
Slips of paper
Several film canisters, small medicine bottles,
  or other small waterproof containers
Kiddie pool or large bucket of water
Toy fishing net

Write one activity, exercise, or game on each slip of paper.
For example, "Run to the nearest tree," "Jump up and down
ten times," "Play tag for five minutes," and so on. Insert each
slip into a separate film canister or other small waterproof
container. Place all the containers
in a kiddie pool. Have your
child use a net to fish
a container out
of the water.
Have him open
it and follow the
instructions.

Independence Day (July 4)

Independence Day celebrates the United States' adoption of the Declaration of Independence in 1776. This holiday is America's birthday. The celebration of Independence Day differs from family to family, but it usually includes a parade, a picnic or barbecue with family and friends, and fireworks at night. Get outdoors and be active with your children as you add some of the following games and activities to your family's Independence Day celebrations.

Duck, Duck, Drip!

This game is suitable for six or more players.

Wet sponge

Have the players sit in a circle. Choose one player to be the goose and give him a wet sponge to hold in one hand. The goose walks around the outside of the circle, tapping players' heads with his other hand and saying *duck* with each tap. When he gets to the player he has chosen as the new goose, he says

drip and squeezes the sponge over the player's head. All the players then jump up; the chosen player chases the goose around the circle while the other players jump in place (or hop, twirl, and so on). The goose tries to reach the chosen player's spot before the chosen player tags him. If the goose succeeds, the chosen player becomes the new goose. If the goose is tagged, he remains the goose for the next round.

Tag Games

If you have a group of children together to celebrate the holiday, teach them a variation or two of this classic game.

- Basic Tag: One child is It. It chases the other players until he tags one. The tagged player then becomes It.
- All-In Tag: One child is It. It chases the other players. Anyone he tags also becomes It and helps chase the remaining players until all have been tagged. The last player tagged becomes the next It.
- Freeze Tag: One child is It. It chases the other players and freezes them by tagging them. A tagged player must remain frozen until an untagged player touches him.
- Hug Tag: One child is It. It chases the other players and until he tags one, who will then become It. Any players who are hugging each other are safe and can't be tagged.

Beanbag Horseshoes

Shovel
Empty, clean large coffee can
4 small beanbags
Paper and pencil (optional)

Dig a small hole in the ground and bury the coffee can so its top is flush with the ground.

Have the first player stand about six feet from the can and try to throw the beanbags into it, one at a time. When he's thrown all the beanbags, retrieve them and, if you like, give two points for each that landed in the can and one point for each that landed near the can. Let the other players take turns throwing the beanbags. The player with the most points wins.

Patriotic Color Race

Several red, white, and blue pompoms, Duplo pieces,
  or small squares of paper
Red, white, and blue baskets (or coffee cans or plastic
  pails covered in colored paper)

Scatter the pompoms over a wide area. Place the baskets randomly in the area. Divide the children equally into three teams and assign each team a color (red, white, or blue). Have the teams stand outside the area. At your signal, have the teams race to pick up the pompoms that match the teams' colors and place them in matching baskets. The team that first places all its pompoms in the baskets wins.

Patriotic Balloon Volleyball

This is a great activity for a large group of children.

Red, white, and blue helium-quality balloons
2 large containers
Badminton net or rope and blanket

Fill the balloons with water and divide them equally into the containers. To create the playing area, set up the net at a height that's level with your child's chest, or string a rope across the court and throw a blanket over the rope. Divide the players equally into two teams, one on each side of the net, and dump a container of balloons on each side of the net. At your signal, the teams pick up their balloons and toss them over the net to the other side. If the balloons don't break, the players on the other team pick them up and toss them back. Play continues until all the balloons are broken or the players tire of the game.

Caution: Balloon pieces can pose an extreme choking hazard for very young children, so any balloon play must be carefully supervised.

Halloween (October 31)

Halloween began in ancient times, and there's great debate over the origins of various aspects of the celebration. One thing is certain, however: People in Europe and North America have celebrated Halloween for many centuries.

This holiday comes as the weather gets colder, days get shorter, and most of our children's activities move indoors. While it's fun and traditional to celebrate Halloween with crafts, baking, trick-or-treating, and pumpkin carving, don't forget to include some lively activities like those that follow in the festivities.

Costume Relay

This activity is suitable for six or more children.

Rope
2 suitcases full of dress-up clothes (old adult-size clothes
or Halloween costumes)

Divide the players equally into two teams. Make a start line with the rope, and have the teams stand behind it with teammates lining up one behind another. Place a suitcase for each team the same distance from the start line. At your signal, the first player from each team runs to his suitcase and puts on everything in it. Have the teams clap and stomp their feet to cheer on their teammates as they run the relay. Once the first player has put on everything, he must remove all the clothes, place them into the suitcase, and run back to his team. The next teammate does the same, repeating until all teammates have had a chance to dress up. The team that finishes the relay first wins.

Spooky Movements

Recording of Halloween music, like Devil's Dance
   by Gil Shaham (optional)

Act out with your child various Halloween scenes and symbols
like the following:
- a black cat arching its back or creeping
- a witch riding a broomstick
- a bat flying
- an owl hooting
- a spider scurrying
- a pumpkin rolling
- a ghost floating

If you like, play *Devil's Dance* to get you in a spooky mood. A great
song for this activity is "Danse Macabre" by Camille Saint-Saëns.

Fill the Pumpkin

Beanbags, rolled-up socks, or balled-up sheets of paper
Plastic pumpkin container

Have your child toss beanbags, rolled-up socks, or paper balls into a plastic pumpkin container. Try the following variations, too:

- Place the pumpkin container on the ground, then on a low table, and then on a higher surface.
- Vary the distance from which your child throws. Have him move closer to the container and farther away.
- Have your child face away from the container and toss the beanbag over his shoulder or between his legs.

Jack-o'-Lantern Catch

Orange balloon
Black marker
Plastic funnel (optional)

Inflate the balloon,
then have your child
use a black marker to
draw jack-o'-lantern features on it. He can hold on to the
spout of a plastic funnel and use it to toss the balloon in the
air and catch it. Two players will enjoy tossing the balloon to
each other or volleying it back and forth.

Caution: Balloon pieces can pose an extreme choking hazard for very young children, so any balloon play must be
carefully supervised.

Spider Scurry

This is a fun activity to do with a group of children.

Action Cube (optional; see Appendix)

Choose one player to be the spider; all the other players are flies. Have the spider stand in the middle of the room while the flies stand on one side. The spider says, "I am the spider." The flies answer, "We are the flies." The spider says, "I'm going to catch you." The flies say, "You just try!" The flies then race to the other side of the room and the spider chases them. Any flies the spider tags must stay in the middle of the room for the next round and help the spider chase and tag the remaining flies. When all the flies have been tagged, choose a new spider and begin again.

Variation: Change the way the spider and flies move for each round (crawling, hopping, skipping, and so on). If you like, roll an Action Cube to determine the movement before beginning a new round.

Shadow Theater

Rope
Light-colored sheet
Bright light

Tie the rope to two objects in the room that can hold the weight of the sheet when it's hung over the rope, like a banister and a heavy floor lamp. Tie the rope at a height above your child's head. Hang the sheet and place a bright light behind it. Have your child stand behind the sheet and act out a Halloween scene or symbol while you try to guess what it is (for example, a witch riding a broom or a werewolf howling to the moon). Take turns acting out movements.

For a group activity, have the children close their eyes while you choose a child to go behind the sheet. The children then try to guess who's behind the sheet as well as the movement being acted out.

Thanksgiving (date varies)

The first Thanksgiving celebration was held by the Pilgrims after their first harvest in 1621. Although many of the original settlers died that first year, the remaining Pilgrims were grateful for the abundance of their harvest and invited their Native American neighbors to join in their three-day feast.

Thanksgiving celebrations today usually include a huge family meal of roast turkey with all the trimmings, which gives you an excellent reason to include lots of physical activity and games in the festivities!

Turkey Trot

Recording of "Turkey in the Straw"

Play the song and do the following activities with your child:
- Make up silly dances to go with the music.
- Strut like turkeys, flapping your wings and gobbling as you go.
- Take turns being a turkey and a farmer. The turkey runs and gobbles with all its might, trying to get away from the farmer who wishes to make it his Thanksgiving dinner!

Pilgrims and Natives

This activity is suitable for six or more children.

Scissors
Construction paper in various colors
Play food (optional)
Magazines (optional)

Cut seasonal food shapes (pumpkins, cornucopias, turkeys, corn, and so on) from colored construction paper. If you like, use play food or pictures cut from magazines instead. Divide the children equally into two teams: the Pilgrims and the Natives. Have the children leave the room while you hide the shapes. When you've finished, have the children return to the room. At your signal, have the teams race to find the most food to bring to the Thanksgiving feast.

Thanksgiving Shape Walk

Scissors
Construction paper in various colors
Magazines (optional)
Painter's tape or poster putty
Basket or other container
Action Cube (optional; see Appendix)

Cut seasonal shapes (pumpkins, cornucopias, Pilgrim hats, turkeys, and so on) from colored construction paper. If you like, use pictures cut from magazines instead. Cut the shapes in half. Attach half of each shape to the wall and put the remaining halves in a basket. Tell your child how you'd like him to move, (hop, skip, jump, run, and so on) or have him roll an Action Cube to determine how he'll move. Have him pick a shape from the basket, then have him move to the wall to match the halves. Help him attach the half to the wall to complete the shape. Continue until he's completed all the shapes.

Pumpkin Fun

1 small pumpkin per player

- With your child on his hands and knees, place a pumpkin on his back. See how far he can crawl before the pumpkin falls off. Two or more players may enjoy doing this activity as a race.
- Have your child walk as fast as he can while balancing a small pumpkin on his head. He may enjoy racing another player to see who can walk the fastest without the pumpkin falling off his head.
- Have your child hold a small pumpkin as he jumps up and down, raises the pumpkin over his head, makes a circle with the pumpkin, and so on.

Pass the Pumpkin

This activity is suitable for four or more children.

1 small pumpkin per player

Have the players stand in a circle. Give one player a small pumpkin and have him begin passing it around the circle. Add another pumpkin and have the players pass it around. Continue adding pumpkins until there are the same number of pumpkins as players. Try to get them to pass the pumpkins faster and faster. If you like, have the players face outward and pass the pumpkins behind their backs, or have them raise their arms and pass the pumpkins above their heads.

Pumpkin Rolling

1 small pumpkin per player
Plastic bowling pin or empty plastic soda bottle
Masking tape

- Have two or more players sit on the floor, facing one another, and roll the pumpkin back and forth.
- Have one child roll the pumpkin across the floor and try to knock over a plastic bowling pin or empty plastic soda bottle.
- Lay tape on the floor. Have your child roll the pumpkin along the tape line as fast as he can.

Hanukkah (dates vary)

Hanukkah, the most joyous and festive of Jewish holidays, lasts eight days and takes place in December—sometimes early and sometimes late in the month.

The Hanukkah celebration is a yearly rededication to the Jewish faith and its traditions. Every year, families gather to light the Hanukkah menorah, remember their ancestors' historic struggle for religious freedom, recite prayers of thanks, exchange gifts, eat special foods, play games, and retell the story of Hanukkah. The following games and activities use some of the special colors and symbols of Hanukkah.

Win the Gelt

Hanukkah traditions include playing games with chocolate coins called gelt.

Masking tape
Beanbag or rolled-up socks
Foil-wrapped chocolate coin

Use masking tape to make a large Star of David on the floor. Have your child stand a few feet from the star and drop-kick a beanbag toward it. Award five points if it lands in the center of the star, two points if it lands in one of the triangles formed by the star's points, and one point if it lands outside the star. Have him run to pick up the beanbag, then run back to the starting point. Tell him to throw the beanbag toward the star while jumping in place, then award points for where it lands. Think of other ways for him to throw the beanbag. Give him a chocolate coin when he reaches a certain number of points.

Elephant Races

Explain to your child that elephants were once used in battle and played a part in the Hanukkah story.

1 chair per team

Divide the children equally into two teams and have the team-mates stand one behind another. Set a chair about fifteen feet away from each team. At your signal, the first player on each team holds his hands together, keeping his arms straight, and bends at the waist. Then he races to the chair, around it, and back to his team, all the time swinging his "trunk." The next teammate in line then runs the race in the same way. Continue until all the teammates have run the race. When a team has finished the race, have them sit. The first team to sit wins.

Variation: Have the children crawl. (This movement may be more appropriate for toddlers.)

Star Walk

Masking tape
Ball, can, or other object to roll

Use masking tape to make a large Star of David on the floor. Have your child use the shape for one or more of the following activities:

- Roll a ball or other object along the outline of the star.
- Walk heel-to-toe along the outline of the star.
- Hop from section to section inside the shape without stepping on the lines.
- Jump from one side to another outside the shape without stepping on the lines.
- Play a game of tag and declare the shape the safe zone.

Dreidel Games

A dreidel is a small spinning top used to play Hanukkah games.

Dreidel (see Appendix to make your own, or use a store-bought one)

Use the dreidel to make up lively games to play with your children. For example, when *S* or *Shin* is up, players sit and stand five times. When *H* or *Hay* is up, the players hop on one foot. *G* or *Gimel* means everyone must crawl around the room, and *N* or *Noon* means players must race to touch a certain object and come back.

Hanukkah Match

Hula-Hoop or yarn or rope
Blue, yellow, and white construction paper
Tape
Blue, yellow, and white containers or boxes
Action Cube (see Appendix)

Place a Hula-Hoop in the middle of the floor or lay yarn in a circle. Roll up the sheets of construction paper and secure them with tape, then set them inside the circle. Place the containers randomly around the room. Roll the Action Cube to determine how your child must to move to the circle (walk, run, skip, and so on), pick up a paper roll, then place it in the matching container. Continue rolling the Action Cube and having your child move the paper rolls until he has placed them all in the matching containers.

Christmas (December 25)

Christmas is a time when Christians celebrate the birth of Jesus Christ. For some, Christmas means the arrival of Santa Claus, Father Christmas, Père Noël, or Saint Nicholas. Christmas celebrations usually emphasize family togetherness, doing thoughtful and loving acts, and good food.

But Christmas often brings with it more than just peace, joy, love, and goodwill. Christmas can be frenzied, stressful, and financially demanding. Add too many late nights, too much rich food, and it's no wonder that we often breathe a sigh of relief when Christmas is over!

The best way to make the most of your Christmas celebration is to forget what everyone else is doing and concentrate on what matters most to you and your family. Spend your time, money, and energy on activities that will build or uphold family traditions and make memories for your child. Don't forget simple pleasures like reading together, making crafts, baking cookies, and sipping hot chocolate together. Spend time outside if you can, or play active indoor games like those that follow to give your child an outlet for his excess energy and excitement.

Christmas Hunt

Construction paper in seasonal colors
6 ice-cream buckets or baskets
Action Cube (see Appendix)
Various kinds of candy (optional)

Cut out six seasonal objects (candy cane, Christmas tree, angel, reindeer, and so on) from construction paper, making two sets of each object. Place the buckets randomly around the room. Using one set of cutouts, place a cutout under each bucket. To play, hold up a cutout from the second set, then throw the Action Cube to determine how your child will move to find the cutout's match (hop, jump, skip, and so on). Your child must move that way to each bucket, lift it up, see if the match is under it, and move on if it's not. Continue until your child has matched all the cutouts.

Variation: For a group activity, use different kinds of candy instead of cutouts. Be sure to provide enough of the candy so each child gets one of each kind.

Holiday Push and Pull

A busy toddler will enjoy this activity.

Plastic soda bottles filled with colored water or sand
Shoebox filled with books and covered with gift-wrapping
Unopened bag of rice placed in a holiday gift bag

Give your toddler the weighted objects one at a time. Challenge him to roll the bottles, push the shoebox, and pull the gift bag a certain distance and within a certain amount of time. Or just let him have fun rolling, pushing, or pulling them on his own.

Holiday Plate Toss

Paper plates with a holiday design
Hula-Hoop or laundry basket

- Have your child throw the paper plates like Frisbees. Have him try to get them into a target, like a Hula-Hoop or a laundry basket placed on the floor.
- Have your child toss the paper plates against the wall. Award one point for plates that land upside down, two points for those that land right side up, and three for those that are left leaning against the wall.
- Have your child try to roll a paper plate on its edge. Compete with him to see whose plate rolls the farthest.

Holiday Shape Hop

Scissors
Construction paper in seasonal colors
Tape
Action Cube (optional; see Appendix)

Cut out seasonal shapes (Christmas tree, star, snowman, and so on) from the construction paper and tape them to the floor. Choose how your child should move: "Hop to the green Christmas tree," "Skip to the yellow star," "Run to the white snowman," and so on. If you like, roll an Action Cube to determine the movement.

Giant Snowball Games

These games are perfect for toddlers.

1 white garbage bag per player
Newspaper
Twist tie

Make a giant snowball by stuffing a white garbage bag with crumpled newspaper and tying it shut. Your toddler will enjoy using it in the following activities:
• Roll the snowball around the room.
• Lift and carry it.
• Kick it.
• Lie on his back and lift the snowball with his feet.

For more than one child, try these activities:
• Play snowball tag. One player is It and must use the snowball to tag another player, who then becomes It.
• Stand in a circle and pass it from child to child as fast as possible.

Indoor Snowball Fun

Several sheets of white paper
Hula-Hoop
Laundry basket
Ping-Pong ball
Empty plastic soda bottle

Crumple up the sheets of paper to make paper snowballs. Then try one or more of the following activities with your child:

- Set a Hula-Hoop on the floor and try to toss the snowballs into the circle.
- Place a laundry basket on a table and try to toss the snowballs into the basket.
- Place a Ping-Pong ball on the mouth of an empty plastic soda bottle, then try to knock off the ball with the snowballs without knocking over the bottle.

Santa's Workshop

This is a terrific Christmas group game.

Beanbags or small packages wrapped in Christmas gift-wrapping

Have one player pretend to be Santa working in his workshop. Santa places several "gifts" (beanbags or packages) nearby him as he works. The other players creep up to Santa, and each tries to steal a gift while Santa works. Santa chases the other players back to a safe zone. If Santa catches a player before reaching the safe zone, that player becomes an elf and must help Santa try to catch players in the next round. When all the players have been caught, choose another child to be Santa and play again.

Christmas Movement

Recording of lively Christmas music
Bells, tambourines, or other rhythm instruments
Crepe paper streamers

- Shake bells and tambourines or other rhythm instruments, wave crepe paper streamers, and dance in time to the music.
- Make up a simple dance to a familiar Christmas song and perform it for the rest of the family.
- Pretend to do winter activities while listening to the music: pull a sled, make a snow angel, ice-skate, play ice hockey, walk in a snowstorm, and so on.

Snowball Fight!

This activity is great for four or more children.

Several sheets of white paper

Crumple up the sheets of paper to make snowballs. Before play begins, create a safe zone to which the children may run. Have one player hide behind a couch or chair with the snowballs, while the other players pretend to ice-skate, ski, or play in the snow. With a shout of "Snowball fight!" the hidden player begins to throw snowballs at the players, who must run to the safe zone before a snowball hits them. If the snowball thrower doesn't hit a player with a snowball, he must return to his hiding place, and play resumes. If a player is hit, he becomes the hidden player.

Holiday Stop and Go

This game is fun to do with a group of children.

Scissors
Construction paper in seasonal colors
Tape
Recording of Christmas music
Action Cube (optional; see Appendix)

Cut out seasonal shapes (Christmas tree, star, snowman, and so on) from construction paper and tape them to the floor. Play Christmas music and have the children move freely around the room. After a while stop the music; each child must run to a shape then freeze. Roll an Action Cube to determine how the children should move when the music begins again, or call out instructions such as, "Children on green Christmas trees must jump," "Children on the white snowmen must hop on one foot," and so on.

Kwanzaa (December 26–January 1)

Kwanzaa is a seven-day African American cultural celebration. The Swahili word *kwanzaa* means "first fruit of the harvest," and the holiday is based on the traditional African winter harvest festival. During this time, African Americans reflect upon the year that's ending and celebrate their African heritage.

Kwanzaa celebrates the harvest and a way of life handed down by ancestors and parents. Special handmade gifts or educational games and books are exchanged, but Kwanzaa emphasizes values rather than gifts. Each day of the Kwanzaa week celebrates one of seven principles or values. These are unity, self-determination, collective work and responsibility, cooperative economics, purpose, creativity, and faith. The following games and activities use Kwanzaa symbols and themes.

Over and Under

Corn is a traditional symbol of
Kwanzaa. This game requires
six or more players and is most
suitable for older preschoolers.

1 ear of corn per team
Large container
Small prizes (optional)

Divide the children equally into two or more teams. Have each
team form a line with teammates standing one behind another
and with their feet shoulders' width apart. Give an ear of corn
to the first player in each line. At your signal, the first players
pass the corn over their heads to the next players, who pass it
between their legs to the next players, who pass it over their
heads to the next players, and so on. The last players in line
run to the front and continue passing. Play continues until
the player who was originally first in line is now the last.
When he receives the corn, he runs to put it into a large container. Then he runs back to his team, and they all sit on the
floor. If you like, award small prizes to the first team to sit.

Variation: If the alternating way of passing the corn from
player to player confuses the children, have them pass the
corn only overhead or only between their legs.

Guard the Garden

This game is suitable for a large group of children. Although African gardens likely yield different crops than your garden, use whatever vegetables you have on hand.

Carrots, potatoes, celery stalks, cucumbers, or other vegetables
Large basket or cardboard box
Whistle or bell (optional)

Place all the vegetables in the basket or box. Choose one player to be the gardener and have him stand beside the vegetables, guarding them. Have the other players stand in a large circle around the gardener. Make sure they're standing at least ten feet from him and are facing away from him. Blow a whistle, ring a bell, or give a command to make the players turn and run toward the vegetables. Each player grabs a vegetable from the basket. As the veggie thieves run back to their spots, the gardener must tag as many as he can. Tagged players must return their vegetables to the basket, and those who make it back to their spots stash their vegetables outside the circle. Have the players take turns being the gardener, and continue to play until all the vegetables have been snatched.

Kwanzaa Movements

If you like, read a book like *Seven Candles for Kwanzaa* by Andrea Davis Pinkney or *K Is for Kwanzaa: A Kwanzaa Alphabet Book* by Juwanda G. Ford, to help you better understand Kwanzaa and give you creative movement ideas.

Recording of traditional African music

- Listen to the music with your child. Physically express how it makes you feel, or make up a dance to go with the music.
- Have your child use his body and imagination to express Kwanzaa themes and symbols like the letter *K*, a candle melting, giving and receiving gifts, eating the Kwanzaa feast, and so on.
- Pretend to be elephants, lions, zebras, giraffes, and other African animals.

Color Balance

The traditional colors of Kwanzaa are black, red, and green.

Strips of black, red, and green fabric

Tie the fabric strips around your child's arms, legs, and head. Keep one strip of each color for yourself. Hold up one strip and have your child move only the parts of his body that have matching strips tied around them. For example, if he has red strips tied around his head and left arm, he could tilt his head to the side and lift up his left arm when you hold up a red strip. Vary the order and speed in which you hold up the strips.

Corn Race

This game requires two or more players.

1 empty egg carton per player
Container of popcorn kernels
Small prizes (optional)

Place each egg carton an equal distance from the container of popcorn kernels. Have each player stand beside an egg carton. At your signal, each player runs to the container, picks up a kernel, runs back to his egg carton, puts the kernel in an empty section, then runs to get another kernel. Tell players to sit when they've filled all their sections. If you like, award a small prize to the first player to sit.

Variation: For several children, divide the children equally into teams and play the game as a relay, using one egg carton per team.

Appendix A

Instructions for Making Props

Action Cube

This simple prop can add fun variety to many of your activities.

1 or 2 single-serving milk or juice cartons
Tape
Plain paper
Pen or marker

Flatten the top of one carton and tape it down securely. Cover the carton with plain paper. On each of the six sides of the carton, write one of the words *walk, run, hop, skip, jump*, and *crawl*. Roll the cube to determine the action to do in activities in the previous chapters.

Or if you like, make another Action Cube. On each of the six sides of the second carton, write one of the words *fast, slow, backward, zigzag, sideways*, and *accelerating*. Roll both cubes together, set a one-minute timer, and have your child do the action that's face-up on one cube and in the manner that's face-up on the other cube. For example, run fast, walk backward, hop sideways, and so on.

Dreidel

A dreidel is a small spinning top used to play Hanukkah games. Follow these directions to make your own dreidel.

Single-serving milk or juice carton
Tape
Plain paper
Pen or marker
Scissors
¼-inch dowel or unsharpened pencil

Flatten the top of the carton and tape it down securely. Cover the carton with plain paper. On each side, write one of the letters *N, G, H,* and *S* or the following Hebrew characters:

Shin Hay Gimel Noon
שׁ ה ג נ

These characters are the first letters in the four words of the Hebrew message *nes gadol hayah sham,* which means "A great miracle happened there." (Hebrew characters are read from right to left.)

Poke a small hole in the centers of the top and bottom of the carton and push the dowel or pencil through both holes to make a spinning top.

Appendix B

Resources for Parents

The games, activities, and other information that make up *The Wiggle & Giggle Busy Book* are gleaned from my years of parenting experience as well as from friends, family members, and other books and resources. The following titles have been helpful to me in planning activities for my own children and looking for the best, most practical ideas and information to include in this book.

Bailey, Guy. *The Ultimate Homeschool Physical Education Game Book: Fun & Easy-to-Use Games & Activities to Help You Teach Your Children Fitness, Movement & Sport Skills*. Camas, Wash.: Educator's Press, 2003.

Boteler, Alison. *The Children's Party Handbook: Fantasy, Food, and Fun*. New York: Barron's Educational Series, Inc., 1986.

Cooper, Kenneth H. *Kid Fitness: A Complete Shape-Up Program from Birth through High School*. New York: Bantam Books, 1991.

Glover, Bob and Jack Shepherd. *The Family Fitness Handbook*. New York: Penguin Books, 1989.

Health Canada. *Family Guide to Physical Activity for Children*. Ottawa, Ont.: Government of Canada, Minister of Health, 2002. (www.healthcanada.ca/paguide)

Hendrick, Joanne. *The Whole Child: Developmental Education for the Early Years*. New York: MacMillan Publishing Company, 1992.

Jackson, Lucy. *Lucy Jackson's Childsplay: Movement Games for Fun and Fitness*. London: Thorsons, 1993.

Kalish, Susan. *Your Child's Fitness: Practical Advice for Parents*. Champaign, Ill.: Human Kinetics Books, 1996.

Mayesky, Mary. *Creative Activities for Young Children, 4th Edition*. Albany, N.Y.: Delmar Publishers Inc., 1990.

McCall, Renee M. and Diane H. Craft. *Moving with a Purpose: Developing Programs for Preschoolers of All Abilities*. Champaign, Ill.: Human Kinetics, 2000.

Miner, Maryalice Fairbank. *Water Fun: Swimming Instruction and Water Games for the Whole Family*. Englewood Cliffs, N.J.: Prentice-Hall Inc.,

Morris, G. S. Don, and Jim Stiehl. *Changing Kids' Games*. Champaign, Ill.: Human Kinetics Books, 1989.

Pica, Rae. *Moving & Learning Series: Preschoolers & Kindergartners*. New York: Delmar, 2000.

Pica, Rae. *Moving & Learning Series: Toddlers*. New York: Delmar, 2000.

Pica, Rae. *Your Active Child: How to Boost Physical, Emotional, and Cognitive Development through Age-Appropriate Activity*. New York: Contemporary Books, 2003.

Sanders, Stephen W. *Active for Life: Developmentally Appropriate Movement Programs for Young Children*. Champaign, Ill.: Human Kinetics, 2002.

Thompson, Myra K. *Jump for Joy: Over 375 Creative Movement Activities for Young Children*. West Nyack, N.Y.: Parker Publishing Company, 1993.

C

D

E

T

Z

Also from Meadowbrook Press

❈ *Busy Books*

The Children's Busy Book, The Toddler's Busy Book, The Preschooler's Busy Book, and ***The Arts and Crafts Busy Book*** each contains 365 activities (one for each day of the year) for your children using items found around the home. The books offer parents and child-care providers fun reading, math, and science activities that will stimulate a child's natural curiosity. They also provide great activities for indoor play during even the longest stretches of bad weather! All four books show you how to save money by making your own paints, play dough, craft clays, glue, paste, and other arts and crafts supplies.

❈ *Mary Had a Little Jam*

Mary Had a Little Jam is the reissue of Bruce Lansky's ***The New Adventures of Mother Goose***, with a completely new title and cover plus four new nursery rhymes and illustrations. ***The New Adventures of Mother Goose*** was a New York Times children's poetry bestseller and #1 title in the "fractured nursery rhymes" category.

❈ *Getting Your Child from No to Yes*

Getting Your Child from No to Yes provides practical, peaceful solutions to the most common preschool behavior problems without fussing or fighting. Readers will find simple, easy-to-use strategies to combat constant dawdling and refusals without losing their cool.

We offer many more titles written to delight, inform, and entertain. To order books with a credit card or browse our full selection of titles, visit our website at:

www.meadowbrookpress.com

or call toll free to place an order, request a free catalog, or ask a question:

1-800-338-2232

Meadowbrook Press • 5451 Smetana Drive • Minnetonka, MN • 55343